About the Author

Diane M. Ross is from Cortland, Ohio and graduated from Youngstown State University (B.S. in Education) and Kent State University (M.Ed. in Special Education and Ed.S. in School Psychology). She worked as a teacher for students with emotional and behavioral challenges, spent time as a United States Peace Corps Volunteer in Southern Africa, and is a current school psychologist. She performs stand-up comedy and Improv when time allows.

Diane lives in Northern Virginia with her wife and two dogs, Camp and Kona.

This is her debut memoir.

First Generation Normal

Diane M. Ross

First Generation Normal

Olympia Publishers
London

www.olympiapublishers.com

OLYMPIA PAPERBACK EDITION

A CIP catalogue record for this title is
available from the British Library.

ISBN: 978-1-80074-229-1

This is a work of creative nonfiction. The events are portrayed to the
best of the author's memory. While all the stories in this book are
true, some names and identifying details have been changed to
protect the privacy of the people involved.

First Published in 2021

Olympia Publishers
Tallis House
2 Tallis Street
London
EC4Y 0AB

Printed in Great Britain

Dedication

For my mom and dad, who gave me the gift of freedom and taught me the value of being authentic. Thank you for providing content that, without which, this book could never happen.

And to the next generation normal, cheers!

Acknowledgements

Special thanks should go to Ms Bridget Doyle for her unwavering encouragement throughout my journey, to Dr Diana Tuggey for critical guidance on my early chapters, and to my wife, Kim Palumbo, for always supporting my creative endeavors.

Part I
Growing Up Free-Range

1
Growing Up Free-Range

By the time I arrived, my mother had already made up her mind. She divorced my father within two years, who by all accounts deserved it, and went back to work full-time. Having already dealt with my brother and sister for the past decade, I suspect she was ready to call it a day. She jumped head-first into the workforce, and my brother and sister were tapped to lead the charge. At ten and eight, respectively, they were The New Order.

I grew up free-range before it was a thing. We had the freedom to live in our natural environment without eyes glaring down upon us, dictating our every move. We learned to be independent because, by and large, people did not do things for us.

It's not to say our parents did not help us with things because they did. They taught us the difference between right and wrong, and that being kind and helpful mattered. They taught us the value of hard work. But most importantly, we were brought up to know and understand natural consequences. That the choices we made might lead to uncomfortable situations. We learned from our mistakes and experiences because they inevitably influenced our future choices. Within this free-range experience, there was also a mutual understanding that there were risks.

It was the 70's — before bicycle helmets and mandatory seat belt laws. Our parents had no problem throwing us in the back of their car and leaving us there while they ran errands. Even in the heat. "Roll the window down if you're hot," my dad would say.

We stood out at the bus stop freezing in the snow and wind without the comfort of sitting in a heated car with our mom or dad. "You're lucky you have a bus — we had to walk to school in this mess!" they would say. And out the door we went in our denim jeans and tennis shoes.

We didn't have waterproof gear like many kids do today. We wore Levi jeans, cotton shirts, and low-top tennis shoes. And they didn't tell us to put a coat on either. Ever. "If you are too dumb to know you should wear a coat, well then you deserve to freeze your ass off," my dad would say.

We carried our schoolbooks by hand. Big, thick textbooks. Nobody thought to buy us a backpack. And we never asked for one. There was no internet, so every bit of schoolwork we did, involved a book, pencil, and paper. Without any online capabilities, there was no evidence to suggest you even had homework. The only way your parents knew you had homework is if you actually told them you did, or you wrote it down somewhere and they saw it.

I didn't have anyone standing over me when I got home, so I rarely opened the book or made any attempts to do homework. It seemed to always be there waiting for me the next day when I got to class, right where I left it.

My earliest memories were of preschool. Because my mom was newly divorced and struggling to provide for us three kids, she worked long hours. I couldn't start preschool until I was potty-trained. So, my mom did what every overworked mother does in a pinch, she put my brother on it.

I remember going into preschool and it was dark. And when I came out of preschool it was dark. Many times, I stayed to have dinner upstairs with the family who ran the day care out of their basement. For years we joked that my picture was on the wall for the longest running stint in the popular preschool. What made it all so memorable to me was that I never knew who was going to pick me up. It was a total crap shoot. Sometimes, although almost never, it was my mother. Otherwise, it was a friend of the family, a neighbor; whoever had a valid driver's license at the time. And even that was not a hard-and-fast-criteria.

But the best was when, out of absolute desperation, she sent my much older and lively cousin, Randy. He was a giant round guy with a beard to match. Probably in his early twenties at the time, he rolled into the preschool parking lot blaring The Allman Brothers, wearing his torn red flannel shirt, holding an open can of Pabst Blue Ribbon beer in one hand and a lit cigarette in the other. He flashed his giant smile at me and off we went.

*

As a kid my world was unpredictable and chaotic; quite literally, a free-for-all and every person for themselves kind of thing. I often found myself in the most unusual situations. And there were no routines or schedules to follow.

Especially with meals. There wasn't any structure to the food we ate. And I don't mean structure like what you see on the Food Network when they look at an amazing gourmet dish and say, "This doesn't make sense." I'm saying that our meals

15

at home, when I was a kid, were entirely random. Haphazard. A real shot in the dark. An afterthought, really.

It wasn't like, well we're having hot dogs for lunch, so let's also have some chips or a vegetable on the side. It was more like, let's eat a half dozen hot dogs and see how we feel. Buns were always optional, as were plates and utensils. If there was still room, maybe we'd squirt some cheese whiz into our mouth or shove a bunch of cookies in just to round it all out.

TV dinners were popular when I was a kid. And to the surprise of many, they also came in breakfast versions.

So, on a typical summer day, I most likely had a frozen breakfast meal that you threw in the oven. Thankfully, we didn't have a microwave back then because I'm pretty sure the oven regulated the pace of my eating. Waiting that extra 24 to 28 minutes probably saved me from gaining inordinate amounts of weight. Otherwise, I would have just thrown something in the microwave every 30 seconds, all day long. Either way, pancakes and sausages were my favorite. And donuts. There was always a box of donuts laying around.

Eventually, lunchtime rolled around and that's when I hit the hot dogs pretty hard. Sometimes I added tater tots just for fun. But mostly, just the hot dogs.

Dinner was always a crap shoot. With my mom's long days at work, she often left meals up to us. But dinner was the one meal that was talked about out loud. As if to say, we know it's a thing, and we should all have it. But to what degree, who is responsible, and under what context will it occur, is another thing entirely. Being the youngest, dinner never fell on my shoulders because I would vote, unanimously, Captain Crunch cereal every time.

My brother often stepped up and made spaghetti. This

usually created an argument because we could never agree on when the noodles were cooked long enough. One day he decided that the noodles were cooked long enough when they stuck to the wall. He took a few of the noodles out of the boiling water and threw them against the wall. "If they stick," he said, "then they're done."

I wanted to try, so I took to throwing them up against the wall too. Some slid down, but most of them stuck. "Yea," I concurred. They seem done."

He used what was left of the noodles to make a giant batch of spaghetti that would, inevitably, sit on the stove for days. I can't say for sure why nobody thought to put it in the refrigerator. But it just sat there. At room temperature. For days. Eventually, it hardened and became an afterthought. Much like the noodles on the wall. I remember walking through the kitchen one time, after having been out on my bike all day, and stopping at the stove. I saw the pot, opened the lid, and thought, why not?

My brother did most of our grocery shopping, which I now know was largely funded by his marijuana plants underneath my mom's bedroom window. Over time, his cooking improved and he gradually adopted unique culinary practices. For example, in an effort to refine his chopping skills, he would take a sharp knife and hack away at the counter tops. He created hundreds of gashes all along the edges. My mom was incredibly unhappy about the hacked-up countertops. But she quickly overlooked his destructive culinary practices after he set the basement wall on fire. "I didn't think concrete could burn like that," he said holding an accelerant of some kind.

Sometimes I'd get hungry in the middle of the night and

rummaged through the refrigerator. One night, I found a white box filled with what appeared to be leftovers. I opened it to find a piece of meat and mashed potatoes. It was the most tender beef I'd ever experienced. It paired nicely with those few large bites of garlic mashed potatoes. It was delicious. This is where my mom was last night? Out feeding her face with amazing food while we fought each other for the last frozen hash brown, I thought wiping my mouth with my pajama sleeve.

What started out as a curious nibble quickly turned into an empty box filled with resentment.

"Who ate my leftovers?" my mom asked the next morning.

"I did," I answered shamelessly.

*

We did have a kitchen table, of course. But we mostly sat in front of the TV while we ate. On the floor. With Gypsy, our very large German Shepherd. Sometimes, Gypsy brought home friends and they also surrounded us on the floor, or roamed the house sniffing out whatever crumbs they could find. They all smelled like a sewer, which made sense because they also roamed free. Whether you believe it or not, sewer is a smell you can become accustomed to. Overlook entirely, even. It becomes familiar. Reminds you of something comforting. A smell that reminds you of home.

Sometimes I was invited to have dinner with the neighbors, which was incredibly kind of them. But that got stressful after a while because there were so many rules to keep track of. Take your shoes off. Wash your hands. Use your inside voice. Sit at a table. Ask to be excused. And they always said a prayer before they ate. I mean, it was all so much to process.

In school, the students in the cafeteria during lunch made their lives sound all organized and functional. Normal even. There was a predictability about their world I didn't understand. They seemed to find comfort in knowing what was going to happen next and there was a confidence about them I couldn't quite hold onto. They always seemed to know what they were having for dinner later that day. They were excited about this or that. Food seemed like a predictable element in their lives. My mom told me years later, we qualified for free and reduced lunches at school, but my brother and sister were too embarrassed, so she never filled out the application. As a result, we just muddled our way through meals from one day to the next. For us, food was a dependent variable. How or when we ate was largely influenced by a variety of circumstances. The better the circumstances, the better we ate. At a time when fitting in mattered, I couldn't imagine chiming in, "Oh, I'll probably just go home and eat some of the spaghetti that's been sitting on the stove for a few days or snack on noodles stuck to the wall."

2
A Wild Child

Growing up free-range meant nobody monitored my play, ever. I don't remember ever learning *how* to play; as in, here are the rules of engagement so be sure to comply with them, and if you don't comply, you'll spend time in a corner somewhere. My play just occurred spontaneously, without oversight, and reaped its own rewards and consequences.

Immediately after school I'd head directly outside to play. The hardest part for me was waiting for everyone to do their homework or change into their 'play' clothes, which I thought was silly and a complete waste of time. I mean, just get outside and play. Some days I wore my play clothes to school and my school clothes to play in. It just seemed more natural and efficient that way, and I never understood why more people weren't on board with that.

I mostly played with the neighborhood kids, which were almost all boys. There were a few girls, but none who really wanted to play sports, army, or ride dirt bikes through the woods. So, I mostly hung with the boys. Two of my neighbors had a lot of rules to follow in their house. They had shoes designated just for outside play. And if they got caught wearing their school shoes outside, they couldn't, as a punishment, come back outside to play. There were times we would just be getting into a good game of something and they would get called in because they had the wrong shoes on, or it was time to eat dinner, or, and this one always threw me, their presence was requested for family time. I never quite knew what that meant. Family time. Don't you live with them? You see them every day. Why designate time for that? I was always trying to get away from my family and I thought other kids would want to do the same.

But the thing is, they had the best toys. I was so jealous of their fake machine guns that made all kind of cool noises. They had real BMX bikes that were bought from a store. And their garage was filled with just about every kind of ball you could imagine.

We didn't have any of those things.

My sister and I were discussing this not too long ago. "Diane, we never had toys growing up," she reminisced.

The thing about my sister is that, when I was a kid, she took to cleaning the house like it was her full-time job. Her vacuum cleaning obsession has become legendary. But it makes sense, if you think about it, because if you don't have any toys to play with, what are you going to do with all of your free time?

I remember asking my dad for a play gun like the neighborhood kids had. "No problem, kid," he said. I must have waited three weeks for it. Finally, he wheeled into the driveway one day after school and excitedly honked the horn. He couldn't wait to show me my new gun. He reached into the backseat and grabbed a brown, wooden, hand-carved gun, and proudly handed it to me.

"It's made out of wood," I said.

"You better believe it's wood, kid," he boasted. "I carved it myself," he said beaming with pride. "And I put a little nail right there on the tip for your view finder," he added.

"But it doesn't make any noise," I said disappointedly.

"The hell it doesn't," he said. He grabbed it out of my hands and started running around the driveway yelling "Pow! Pow! Pow!'

Later that night I walked over to the neighbors, who all had their fancy guns out and were getting ready to play a game. I casually walked up to them, holding my wooden play gun down by my side.

"What's *that*?" they asked laughing.

"My new gun. My dad made it," I told them.

"Oh man, that's terrible. Do you want to borrow one of ours?" one of them asked.

I sighed deeply, knowing my dad was going to ask me if I played with it, and then remind me that it took him three weeks to make.

"No." I said begrudgingly. "I'm fine."

It was the worst game of my life. My "Pow! Pow! Pow!" was immediately overtaken by their multitude of machine gun sounds. One of them came up to me and just pointed their gun right in my face, "Dadaddaadsa Bbllahhhdaba! You're dead!"

No shit, I thought.

*

A few months later, having not learned my lesson, I asked my dad for a new BMX bike like the neighborhood kids had.

"I can't keep up with them on this stupid thing," I said pointing at my purple bike with a banana seat. "I need a real BMX bike!" I demanded.

"No problem, kid," he said. He snatched it right out of my

hands, put it in the back of his station wagon, and tore out of the driveway.

This time, I waited a lot longer. Almost a month went by. Then, finally, he rolled into the driveway one day and shouted out of the window, "I gotta' bike for you, kid!"

But I could sense some hesitation as he pulled it out of the station wagon. "Listen," he said, "I made some modifications to your old bike." I know it's not new, but just... just... hear your 'ole man out, kid." He proceeded to show me all the new upgrades. A new coat of matte black paint. A BMX bike seat. Black pedals. Gone were the handlebar streamers and reflectors. "Reflectors are for sissies anyhow," he said.

"But it's the same bike!" I screamed back at him.

"Just give it a chance. Ok? Can you do that?" he asked.

Soon after, the neighbor kids all rolled up my driveway on their BMX bikes and asked if I wanted to go riding in the woods. I ran into the garage and pulled out my not-so-new bike.

"What's *that*?" they asked.

"I guess my dad made some upgrades," I answered.

"Ok, well let's go!" they all shouted.

And off we went. But instantly, I fell behind because it was the *same* bike as before. Nothing had changed. It may have *looked* different, but one fact remained. I still couldn't keep up.

They hit the trail way ahead of me and when I finally caught up to them, they were racing down the hills, hitting the jumps, and spinning out at the bottom.

Wow, I thought. I had never been to that part of the woods before and I watched them for a while, just crushing it on their BMX bikes.

"C'mon!" one of them shouted from the bottom of the hill. I couldn't hold back any longer, so I took off, but as soon as I hit the first jump, I knew I was in for it. The front end of my bike immediately lifted in the air because it was not, in fact, a BMX bike; but rather, a little girl's purple bike that used to have a banana seat and handlebar streamers. The black paint and BMX seat were not going to save me.

The bike was so light that as soon as it hit the mound of dirt, the front end flipped up and I fell back, and off the bike entirely. I landed hard and rolled a few times before watching the bike fly through the air, crashing into the adjacent gulch.

I didn't sustain any lasting injuries, thankfully, and my dad felt pretty bad about the accident. For my next birthday, I couldn't have been more surprised when I got a shiny, new silver Mongoose BMX bike. It was sweet. And purchased at full price, from an actual store.

*

As a kid I had the best backyard in the neighborhood. There were three trees that were perfectly aligned to represent first, second, and third base, with a giant dirt circle for home plate. It was perfect for kickball, football, or Smear the Queer.

If you don't know Smear the Queer, it's a game that you could never get away with playing today. First, it's offensive as hell. Second, it's an inherently violent game that preys on the weakest kid. It's just overall terrible. Having said all of that, it's pretty simple to play. You just throw the ball up in the air and whoever catches it runs for their life until they get *smeared,* or aggressively tackled and buried underneath a heavy pile of bodies. Also, everyone calls you queer while your face is smashed into the dirt. To be clear, I don't think I fully understood the meaning of queer as a kid. I certainly didn't suspect that *I* was queer. But I did know that to be queer in the game was bad, and so we avoided it at all cost.

We had firm rules about the games we played, but of course modified them as needed. Anything into the neighbor's yard was a home run or automatic double, depending on how competitive we were feeling.

And we used ghost runners if we were short on players. We didn't let someone being grounded disrupt the game; we just gave them a ghost runner. Sometimes we argued about how fast the ghost runner was, based on whoever it was ghosted after.

One thing about growing up free-range is that if you had a problem while playing, there was nobody around to help you mediate it. You had to figure it out all on your own. Sometimes, we hashed it out with words over a game of kickball. "You can't just call a ghost runner because you don't *feel* like running any more!"

"Yea, that's stupid!" someone would say.

And when words failed, sometimes you just hauled off and pushed a kid. Or punched them in the face. And that either settled the mess, or they pushed you back, or punched you even harder. This may have sent you home crying. Forced you into hiding in a closet somewhere until it all died down. You might not talk for a few days. But neighbors are a lot like family in that you can't pick them, and you're stuck with them until they die or move away. So, you get over it. Move on. And eventually play together again.

*

Without any real supervision or accountability, I found myself in all sorts of precarious situations.

The first time I was pulled over by the police I was wearing an incredible hulk T-shirt, shorts, and tennis shoes. The over-sized matte black motorcycle helmet I was wearing sat crooked on my head. I was pedal to the metal and every time I hit a bump the helmet slid down over my face. I constantly had one hand on the steering wheel and the other on my helmet. The dust was swirling around, and the partially paved road kicked up gravel that seemed to complicate the situation.

I never saw the lights because I didn't have a rear-view mirror. And I never heard the sirens because of the loud engine and my apparent hearing loss.

So, when a police car suddenly pulled in front of me and hit the brakes, I was obviously surprised. Also, I was eight, and didn't understand the rules of the road.

*

To start with, it was my father's idea. For Christmas earlier that year, he bought me a bright red Go-Kart. I remember it perfectly. We were all sitting in the living room in a ranch style house that sat on a mixed gravel/paved road out in the country. My parents were divorced so the Christmas agreement was that we could open our stockings but had to wait for my dad to arrive before opening gifts. Most of the time, he showed up fairly early, arms loaded with presents. Sometimes, though, he arrived late morning or early afternoon. He didn't have a telephone, so we never knew what time he would arrive.

To be fair, my dad doesn't love Christmas. In fact, he despises it. But when we were kids, he *did* Christmas. And he always showed up no matter what was going on with him.

One time he walked into the house with more than a handful of gifts. He had a black eye, broken nose, and a few broken ribs.

"You should see the other guys," he told us as he gingerly put his presents under the tree.

The story is that he confronted some guys about loud music and one thing led to another. Because my dad never backs away from a challenge, he leaned into the mess, but they clearly leaned in harder.

My dad will tell you he was jumped by two six-foot guys, but all his barroom buddies say it was more like six two-foot guys.

Either way, I remember he made a drink shortly after he arrived, fell back into the chair and held the cold glass up to his face. It seemed like a real rock bottom moment for him and I'd like to think he was staring at the Christmas tree, contemplating his life's choices. That maybe he thought about how his appearance might scare his kids.

Never before had I seen my dad look so down on his luck. A real train wreck. Homeless, even. But we were all generally un-phased by his appearance. It was just another Christmas morning as we all took turns re-filling his glass.

*

On the Christmas morning of the Go-Kart reveal, he put all of the presents down under the tree. I rushed over but didn't see any for me. Confused, I desperately looked around, shoved

27

packages out of the way, and whimpered ever so slightly. Then, out of nowhere, he wheeled a bright red Go-Kart into the living room. It was amazing.

My mother, on the other hand, was livid. As she was the one who lived with me full time, she absolutely knew this was a terrible idea. To make matters worse, he made some modifications to the thing.

"I took the governor off for you," he said proudly. "That's what keeps your speed down, those bastards," he said. "You should have no problem going full throttle here, kid," he boasted.

It seemed like everything I had ever dreamed of was coming alive.

But within minutes of my first ride, I flipped it over entirely, trapping myself under the thing. The engine still roaring. Tires spinning. My head smashed into the ground. Unable to free myself, I screamed for help until my brother arrived on the scene. My dad was a few steps behind him, and together they got me right side up. I ran into the house crying, but my dad marched me right back out to the Go-Kart, slapped my brother's old dirt bike helmet on my head, and pushed me off again.

After that terrifying incident, I managed to gain some confidence and, within weeks, I was zipping around all fast and furious with my new wheels. I tore around the neighborhood, carving huge ruts into the yard, and threw riders off with my sharp turns.

*

So, on that fateful day, when I was stopped on the side of the road, a policeman, a Sheriff to be exact, got out of his car and walked back to me.

"Do you know who I am?" he asked.

Of course I don't, I thought. I was just a kid riding in a Go-Kart on the road with no parental supervision. And he was a police officer in a very important car with lights and sirens.

"No," I said.

"I'm Sheriff Stotts," he said. "I'm your great uncle," he continued.

"Oh," I said not recognizing him at all. "You called my mom?" I asked.

"I'm about to," he said walking back to his car.

Every now and then, while I waited on the side of the road, a car passed by and the dust swirled up around me. I finally shut the Go-Kart off because he was taking a very long time. I had been having trouble with the chain, so I got out to take a look at everything.

What he learned on that phone call was that my mom was in the hospital after a major surgery. I can't say for sure who was supervising me at the time. But truth be told, my mom probably deserved a break from it all. I'm pretty sure the phone call from the Sheriff while she lay in her hospital bed probably disrupted any break from parenting that she had hoped for.

He walked back to me and said, "I can't let you drive this back down the road by yourself and I'm too big to fit in it to drive it for you, so you'll just have to drive and I'll follow behind you."

*

After the police escort home, I was told to lay low on the Go-

29

Kart for a while, for some fairly obvious reasons, and encouraged to channel my energies into a new activity.

*

Because I had to stay a little closer to home, I decided to make some good use of the fort my dad built for us in the garage. It was entirely hand-crafted by him, hung from the rafters, and consumed almost the entire back wall of our garage. Had you walked into to our garage, as a stranger in 1978, your eyes would immediately be drawn to the over-sized hanging wooden structure and think, who lives in *that*?

There were a half dozen two-by-fours nailed into the wall studs so you could climb up and down to get in and out of the thing, and it had a lockable trap door on the far left side that you could throw a rope out of and slide down in an emergency. What that emergency might be, I had no idea. But I can tell you that I spent the better part of three days preparing for it. A ghost invasion. The police closing in on me after a wild Go-Kart chase. A blazing fire soaring through the garage. A hungry school of sharks below waiting to devour my chubby body.

The fort was home to a host of my imaginary play ideas. I was an FBI agent tracking bad guys. Or, I was a bad guy hiding out from the evil FBI agents. I fathomed up wildly obscure plots where I was running to or from a fiery crisis, with a spitfire attitude and haphazard plan, facing complex scenarios that only I, alone, could manage.

I stashed snacks in the cut-out cubby just in case I had to hide out for a particularly long period of time or make a triumphant run for it. Just in case.

Truth be told, while nobody was paying much attention, I

slowly started moving into the fort. I brought some clothes. A few of my toys. Pens and paper to write notes or draw. I even tried to make a vest for my dog, Gypsy, so I could hoist her up to the fort with me. Without realizing it, I was slowly establishing a one-room studio apartment for myself. I invited friends over, like it was an 8-year-old cocktail party. I offered them appetizers of dried cereal and potato chips, and a cup of Sunny Delight to wash it all down. I invited them to use my secret cubby for whatever they might want to store, for future hypothetical events. I led them into my imaginary world, where anything was possible.

I donned elaborate outfits to go along with my imaginative play. For days, I'd run around wearing a cowboy hat, boots, and a holster, which housed my shiny, Lone Ranger cap gun. If I was feeling sporty, I'd walk around the house in my football helmet and shoulder pads, bumping into anything that stood still. If I didn't feel like playing football, I'd steal my brother's perfectly pinstriped baseball uniform, which was about three sizes too large, and spend hours perfecting my baseball slide into the home plate in our backyard.

On weekends, when things were slow, I'd stay with my dad in the city. I'd wake up on Saturday morning and head outside to run the streets with the neighbor kids. They were very different from my neighbors at home. They were older and wilder. And dirtier. There was a scrappiness to them I couldn't relate to. Like, they had nothing more to lose. Whatever I thought my family lacked, they lacked more of it. They didn't have all the fancy toys my neighbors at home had. In fact, I don't recall seeing many toys at all. And I'm sure they sensed that I was also different. Less desperate. And in some weird way, hopeful for some kind of future. At least as much as a little kid can be. I was game for just about any adventure, so they let me hang out with them. We zipped around the alleys. Jumped backyard fences. Ran from stray dogs. Threw metal garbage can lids at each other like frisbees. Played on the train tracks. One kid, wild as the day was long, took to shooting at us with his BB gun. We never knew what corner he would pop out of, and just 'POW'. We dodged BB's like our lives depended on it. Which as it turns out, kind of did.

My dad didn't like me playing with the city kids for some fairly obvious reasons. One time, he caught me playing with matches in a back alley. I never saw him coming. He was like a turkey vulture plucking a chicken out of a backyard. Swift and purposeful. He proceeded to drag me, kicking and screaming, down the middle of the street. My feet barely touched the ground, and he whaled on my backside every few steps. The thing about my dad is that he is a big guy with extraordinarily long arms. And completely unfiltered when he's angry. He's not someone you want to piss off in a back alley. Or ever, actually.

He was swinging at me so haphazardly I couldn't make out what direction the blows were coming from. It was a lot like being attacked by a pissed-off orangutan. I couldn't escape him no matter how hard I tried.

The whole thing caught me completely off guard because my dad had never hit me before. He just had a way about him that let you know he disapproved without ever laying a hand on you. His nostrils flared and he would posture up, flailing those orangutan arms like he was about to unleash a giant can of whoop ass. And that was enough for me to settle right down. Get out of his line of sight. But after the whaling, I couldn't help but feel betrayed. I thought he understood me. That we were a thing. Two peas in a pod. That I could come into the city with him and we could run wild together. But this was *betrayal.* Suddenly there were rules that I didn't understand and it all just happened so fast.

In hindsight, I suspect tensions were running high on account of my brother almost burning the house down and all. So, it makes sense to me, now, that my dad saw me playing with matches and just completely lost his shit.

I eventually stopped playing with the city kids, right around the time one of the boys fell from a train trestle and the BB gun boy went to juvie.

It's also right around the time my dad got me a bike to keep at his house. Every Saturday morning, if we didn't go out on the boat, we rode our bikes all over the city. Without helmets. Yelling back and forth to each other about this or that. We jumped curbs. Dodged traffic. Played tag, on our bikes, in empty parking lots. And hung our Saturday night snacks from the handlebars as we peddled home.

If the weather was nice, my dad would gather some nearby wood and start a fire for us behind the house. To be clear, it wasn't the house we slept in; but rather, the vacant house across the street that had recently been engulfed in flames. He decided to buy the house as-is. *After* the fire. He didn't want the house when it was still inhabitable, but something clicked for him after the fire. It's as if he said, "Wait, it just burnt down? Well, that changes everything! Yes, I'll take it."

It didn't have much curb appeal unless you had a thing for the charred look. For the most part, it survived the recent fire. But it had substantial damage. Some of the windows were busted out and the inside was essentially gutted. But the doors were still intact and lockable. He boarded up the windows,

33

installed new locks, and turned it into an oversized tool shed.

We'd sit around a makeshift fire pit, ignoring the barbed wire-enclosed trucking company parking lot behind us, and enjoyed the flames. When the fire needed more fuel, my dad casually walked over to his new tool shed, ripped some wood off, and drug it back over to the pit. It might have been a shudder, loose piece of siding, or a floorboard. It was hard to tell. And if he struggled to get anything going at all, he just took out a giant plastic container of lighter fluid and doused the hell out of it.

Late into the evening he would eventually let the fire die down, and we walked back across the street to the inhabited house and settled ourselves in for some black and white television.

My dad told me about the boys' fate just before The Benny Hill Show came on. If you don't know the show, it was one of the most absurdly vulgar, and undeniably, most risqué shows on television at the time. It was one hundred percent not suitable for children. As evidenced by it being aired at midnight. Anyway, he told me the news of the boys, just before the show. As if to say, it all starts with matches in a back alley, kid, and playing with them leads to severe injury and incarceration. I tried to let that all sink in while I watched him shovel potato chips and dip into his mouth, washing it all down with a handful of beers. I watched him laughing, spitting chips out of his mouth, gurgling, "This is so raunchy, kid. You shouldn't be watching it."

Even my young brain saw the irony in it all. And I thought, yea, I'm sure it all starts with playing with matches in a back alley.

3
A Latchkey Kid

Growing up free-range meant that I never knew if anyone would be home after school. It was all just so unpredictable. As a result, some people called me a latchkey kid, which is a young child who, due to parents working outside of the home, let themselves into the house after school using a key they wore around their neck, or attached to some other part of their body. I seemingly fit that description. But I wasn't a latchkey kid. At least not in the literal sense. Mostly because that means I would have had an actual key to get into the house after school. I never had a house key hanging around my neck. Or in my pocket. Or even hidden under a door mat somewhere. Because we generally just left the doors unlocked entirely. They were completely wide open for relatives, neighbors, friends of the family, or for anyone needing a respite as they moved along on their journey.

But mostly, we left the doors unlocked for our revolving door of babysitters. Cathy, Jill, Lori, Shauna, Rebecca, Jenny, Brianna, and the entire McConnoly clan of girls — five to be exact. They each made their way into our house and did the best they could with what they had to work with. On any given day, one of them might be on the clock when I walked through the front door, sitting on the long, green couch we acquired from Goodwill, smashed up against the back wall of the living room. Watching a soap opera. Or reading a magazine.

"Who are you?" I asked walking through the front door. She didn't look much older than my sister.

"Lori," she said chomping on her gum. "Your babysitter," she finished.

"Oh. Well, I'm about to go play outside so you're free to go," I said all adult-like.

The babysitters never lasted very long though. It seemed like just as I started to learn their name and get attached, they would disappear. I suspect my brother tried to date a few of them, which didn't go over very well. But given the long list of names my sister still remembers to this day, my mom made sure to have a deep bench so there was always another one waiting in the wings.

*

Sometimes there wasn't a babysitter on the clock and the door got mistakenly locked. It wasn't locked out of an abundance of caution or anything, but more like a hand got a little too familiar with the doorknob and a switch was accidentally flipped. In those cases, there was only one way to get into the house. We crawled in through my mother's bedroom window.

This was fine when we were younger, and smaller. As the youngest, I was always being hoisted up by my brother or sister and shoved in through the window. But as we got older, and I got chubbier, we had to solicit the help of our much tinier neighbor, Janet. It's not to say that I didn't still *try* to let myself in when nobody else was around. When feeling up for the challenge, I would push aside my brother's blooming marijuana plants, stand on the large rock beneath my mother's bedroom window, and desperately try to lift myself up, scraping and grasping for the window seal, just enough to open the window.

Thankfully, most of the screens in the house had been torn out or broken, so that wasn't an unnecessary obstacle to deal with. I held onto the ledge, while my knees and feet dug hard into the side of the house like my life depended on it. My elbows worked double time, trying desperately to both lift and shove my chubby self through the window. I certainly gave it a strong go, to the point where I was teetering on my mid-section like a seesaw at the playground. My ass and legs dangled out of the window for the whole world to see, while my front half sought the comfort of my mom's bed on the other side, and a clear path to the refrigerator just down the hall. The seesaw move was the point of no return; whereby, I was forced to muster all of my inner strength for that final lunge forward, finally flailing myself head-first onto the bed.

But when I felt like I didn't have all of that it in me, I just walked across the yards to ask Janet to help.

Her mom would faithfully answer the door, and I would ramble on and on about this or that, explaining to her why I was curiously locked out of the house. I'd then sheepishly ask if I could borrow her daughter to shove her through my mom's bedroom window.

"Sure, let me get her for you," she always replied.

I remember lifting her up and shoving her in through the window, then walking around to the front door to greet her as she opened it from the inside.

"Thanks," I'd say.

"Sure, want to play?" she'd ask.

And off we went.

Sometimes I'd come home after school to find that my brother's friends had let themselves in and decided to get high in the basement while they waited for him to get home from school or work. He also had a girlfriend, who turned out to be incredibly wild. Although she wasn't officially a babysitter; she was, by far, my favorite after-school character. She was always up for playing games and going out on adventures with me.

She loved my Go-Kart and we were always out riding around on it. One day, she got a little out of hand and drove it all the way into town. I remember holding on tight, screaming as she weaved in and out of traffic. Or rather, as traffic weaved in and around us trying not to kill us. It hadn't been that long since I got pulled over by the Sheriff, so I knew being on the road was bad news. I tried telling her that, but she was in another world. I'll never forget her crazy face. Eyes and mouth wide open, and her wildly blonde curly hair blowing around in the wind.

My screaming must have really gotten on her nerves because on the way back home she just suddenly pulled the thing over to the side of the road, skidded to a complete stop, and yelled, "Get out!"

So I did. And I watched her drive off in *my* Go-Kart, all by herself, with that wild hair blowing in the wind. I had to walk the rest of the way home.

I suspect she was pretty high on something because, well, most of my brother's friends were. Not long after that incident, something dramatic must have happened because she just stopped coming around. Even though nobody would talk about it around me, it made me feel sad. I really liked hanging out with her, despite being kicked off of my own Go-Kart. I *was* pretty loud about the whole thing, so I don't blame her much for that. Plus, she was high and all, which makes even more sense now.

*

If it wasn't a babysitter or my brother's friends, I might come home to find our gun-toting neighbor, Mr Straud, Janet's father, who was there in response to my sister's pleas for help if she thought she heard a noise. That guy was always on call. And entirely used to seeing us standing on his front porch, late at night, in our socks, sometimes soaking wet if it was raining, panting from the sprint across the yards.

"We… uh… we… heard something… in… the… hallway," we managed to get out in between pants.

"Ok, come on in," Mr Straud said reassuringly. "You all wait right here," he said walking back to get his rifle.

And we'd watch through their large picture window as he marched across the yards with his long gun, wearing just his underwear, nightshirt, and work boots.

The guy had a family of his own but thought nothing of it to take off on a whim to protect three more kids who didn't even belong to him. Of course, he never found any perpetrators. Just things that had fallen or been knocked over by my brother's friends climbing in and out of his bedroom window. It's a good thing Mr Straud didn't catch any of them in action. Or if he did, he never said anything about it. None of them seemed to have gotten shot anyway.

Probably one of the strangest visits occurred one day when I came home from school and my mom was sitting at the kitchen table talking to a woman I didn't recognize. She introduced her only as, "the nice lady from Children's Services." Weird, I thought. I wondered what kind of services she was going to offer us.

My mom leaned into to me and said, "It appears someone called Children's Services after seeing you climb through my bedroom window after school last week."

"Oh that?" I replied. "Yea, the front door was locked," I said matter-of-factly.

"Well, this lady would like to ask you some questions," my mom went on.

A quiz? I just got out of school. What kind of nonsense was this? I wondered.

What transpired that afternoon was wildly out of the ordinary, even for us. We weren't used to having people check in on us and ask such intrusive questions. But I did my best to answer them. Yes, I felt safe. Yes, we had food.

Sensing the seriousness of the situation, I fought off the urge to say, I especially feel safe when our neighbor comes over with his rifle and, oh look, there's a noodle right there on the wall. We got it all covered so you can go now.

Shortly after the visit, we learned that it was one of my dad's friends who was driving by the house at the exact time I was crawling through the window. He told my dad about what he saw, which set off some alarm in his head that he needed to suddenly get involved. It was a cheap shot really. He couldn't just sit back while his kids were climbing through windows and running amuck. That didn't look good for him. He even threatened to file for custody of us. To be clear, he didn't *want* custody of us. He just wanted the appearance of it.

Either way, no more climbing through the windows, my

mom told me. And I got a real house key, which I lost repeatedly. For a little while my mom was home more, so there was a lull in babysitters and chaos. She took a side job doing bookkeeping at our kitchen table. I remember the adding machine running for hours, and she would meticulously write numbers in neatly organized rows. On those days, she cooked dinner for us, and it was nice. It felt calm. Normal, even.

But eventually, she went back to working full-time outside of the house, and I officially became a Latchkey Kid. I tried my best to keep my key safe and not climb through any more windows.

4
Sunday Visitation

Growing up free-range with divorced parents meant a lot of spontaneous visits with my dad.

There wasn't a formal custody agreement, as far as I could tell. I suspect that would have required them to sit down, make a plan, and stick to it. Naturally, this didn't align with their parenting inclinations. So, at some point, they must have just decided to wing it. Play it by ear. Figure things out as they went.

While my mom hustled during the week to keep us alive, my dad mostly reserved parenting for the weekends. Well, most weekends anyway. It's not to say he *never* came by during the week because he did. During the summer, he picked us up for boating almost every day of the week. Although by the time my brother and sister hit double digits in age, they were pretty much over his antics, and declined the invitations. I don't blame them for that, actually, because he was pretty exhausting. I hadn't quite gotten tired of him yet; or rather, I just didn't know any better. Either way, he was left with just me.

And it's not like he visited *every* Sunday, because he didn't do that either. To be honest, his visits were pretty hit or miss. There were no rules or expectations around pick-up and drop-off. When he picked me up, there was no formal return policy. I just had to be home at some point before school the next morning.

Some Sundays he no-showed entirely. No call. No visit. Just radio silence. And then on other Sundays, he might no-show, but call late in the day saying, "Yea, kid, the day got away from me."

I say all of that to say, Sunday visitations with my father turned into a decade long adventure that always kept me on my toes. Sundays became the day I never knew what to expect.

*

Like the time he showed up and said he wanted to teach me how to drive. I was ten. He drove me to the town's cemetery, saying, "This is a great place to learn how to drive because everyone here is already dead."

He put me on his lap and taught me how to drive.

Every time I jumped into his raggedy old car it was always an adventure.

"I gotta' hit the junk yard, kid," he would start off. And so we went.

He would be looking for whatever it was he was looking for and I would wander aimlessly amongst the giant piles of tin structures I did not recognize.

"Nobody goes to junkyards any more," he would say while admiring a shiny piece of junk. "They just want to buy everything new."

It was during these moments that I learned about nuts, bolts, and an assortment of car parts that, as it turns out, has not helped me at all in life. And I was introduced to the kind of characters that go to junkyards. They're not always the kind of people you might interview to be a babysitter. But they seem to possess a kind of character worth knowing.

If the weather was nice, he would pick me up and we'd drive down to the lake and people watch. It was one of his favorite pastimes. We'd sit on the docks at the boat ramp and watch people load or unload their boats in or out of the water.

"This is where divorces start, kid," he'd say laughing. And he would proceed to critique each boater, carefully analyzing each and every move like a chess match, commenting on what they were doing right or wrong, and predicting the potentially disastrous outcome.

*

"See that?" he asked pointing toward a boat half-way in the water. "He didn't go back far enough so the boat isn't going to slide off like it should," he said shaking his head. "That's more work for his wife. Look at her face right now," he added.

"Or right over there, Jesus Christ, are you watching this?" he would say elbowing me in the ribs. "This guy doesn't want to get wet so he's standing on the hitch and tongue of the trailer — watch him slip off — wait for it," he said all suspenseful. "It's just a matter of time… he's getting nervous now… look at his face… look at all of these other boats trying to come in… he can't crank the handle at that angle… look it's getting in his head…"

And then, SPLASH!

He erupted with laughter. "So much for not getting wet!" he said loudly. And the guy looked over at us.

It reminded me of the time my dad got into an argument with another boater. We were coming in from a long day of water skiing. It was just my brother and I with him in the boat.

My dad and this other guy were both vying for a spot on the dock, and they started having words with each other, and then the guy told my dad to get out of the boat so they could, "handle it like men." My dad's nostrils were fully flared as he cursed him up and down. He finally docked the boat, got in my brother's face, and told him he better be five steps behind him with the paddle, just in case it came to that. My brother couldn't have been more than fifteen at the time, but followed him right out of the boat, paddle in hand.

That's the thing about my dad. You don't have time to think about what he's asking of you. By virtue of simply being next to him, you unknowingly agree to whatever chaotic events unfold. You might have to stop at the county dump before going to lunch. Wrangle a trapped raccoon on your way to a family get together. Or stand tall on a dock with a canoe paddle.

So, after the guy fell into the water, and my dad laughed out loud at him, I slowly inched myself away from him because I wasn't trying to be yelled at to go find a paddle, just in case it came to that.

*

As far as Sunday visitations go, I can't really complain that he never took me to normal places like the mall, because he did. All of my friends seem to do normal things like go shopping at the mall. Or they went out to dinner as a family. I was always envious of that. Because when we went to the mall, all we did was ride the escalators. For hours. Up and down. Sometimes, I'd get bored and run up the down escalator. That was pretty exciting. But I don't remember him ever buying me anything.

We pretty much did whatever was mall-related and *free*. I don't remember him buying any food either. After the mall excursion, we usually drove around to visit various people we knew or were in some way related to.

"Maybe we can get a meal off of them, kid," he'd say pulling into their driveway.

*

Him letting me walk around a junkyard by myself for hours as a kid, teaching me to drive at the age of ten in a cemetery, and pushing me into the middle of a boating altercation probably concerns you. And it should. Because they are all inherently unsafe. One small puff of wind, wrong turn, or intoxicated boater, and I could have been dead. But if it's one thing about my dad, he has always fundamentally believed that unique characters and situations make you a better person.

5
A Girl and Her Doghouse

My siblings and I were tight through it all. We had each other's backs, mostly. When we were very young, my brother and sister used me like a toy. They shoved me through a small hole down a metal chute and into a wooden clothes hamper. I started on the top floor and slid down the chute into the basement. At first, I landed in a pile of dirty clothes in the hamper. That was pretty fun. But the hamper eventually wore weak. After one overly aggressive push from them, I flew down the chute and blew right through the bottom of the hamper, landing hard on the concrete floor below. I cried, and my mom yelled at them.

Another time, when I was in my baby walker, they spread out in the kitchen. One of them sprayed the linoleum floor with Pledge, which turned a normal kitchen floor into a dangerous sheet of ice. They were pushing me back and forth like a game of shuffleboard. My little feet were dangling trying desperately to keep up with the wheels. Back and forth. Then, one push too hard and someone missed me, and I crashed into the five-gallon glass water jug in the corner, smashing it into the wall and shattering. Glass and water went everywhere. Again, I cried, and my mom yelled at them.

For the most part, my brother and sister kept an eye on me. There were a few times, however, where they completely dropped the ball.

One summer day, we had been out on the boat all day with my dad. My brother didn't come along, so it was just my dad, me, my sister, and her best friend, Sheila. My dad pulled the boat out of the water and parked it along the edge of the large parking lot. I always liked to stay in the boat when he drove it out of the water and through the parking lot because it made me feel like superman floating across land. We were parked, and he was busy tying things down. "Ok, kid, get out of the boat now," he yelled from the rear.

During the summer, I was just a chubby kid who ran around in a one-piece bathing suit and tennis shoes, all the time. Nobody ever thought to cover me up, or at least tell me to put some shorts on. So, there I was, standing in a boat parked on land, wearing my one-piece bathing suit and tennis shoes, preparing to slide over the edge. I had done it a hundred times. I knew the drill. Throw one leg over, turn onto my stomach, hold the windshield, gradually drop my body until my chubby little leg landed on the wheel guard. Then flip back around and leap off.

This time, I must have mis-calculated my position because when I threw my one leg over, my bathing suit got caught on the metal cleat, forcing me to lose my balance and slide down just enough to rip my suit, but not entirely enough to break me free. I was stuck, in mid-air, being held up only by the threads of my bathing suit. Because my hefty body was dangling in mid-air the suit was being stretched to the max, forcing my chubby butt cheeks and girl parts to hang out for the whole world to see. All four of my limbs were waving wildly in the air and I was squealing like a stuck pig trying to escape death.

My sister and her friend arrived on the scene and instead of helping me off the cleat, they fell to the ground laughing hysterically, which made me cry even harder. They eventually did try to help me, but I was too heavy for them, and what with all the laughing, they were completely useless.

The whole scene lasted what seemed like an eternity, until my dad came to my rescue. "Jesus Christ! How the hell did you do this!" he shouted as he lifted me off the cleat.

He yelled at me like I suddenly decided to just hang myself on a metal cleat, *on purpose.* Like I had nothing better to do with my time.

Then he turned to my sister and let her have it. Boy, was he pissed. But she couldn't stop laughing, which made him even more angry.

On the car ride home, after he calmed down about the whole thing, he looked back at me in the rearview mirror and said, "Don't worry, kid, we'll get you a new suit."

As if losing the suit was at the forefront of my mind.

*

Another time, when I was still very young, I awoke from a bad dream and cried out for my mom. But she didn't come. I lay in bed crying and calling out for my brother and sister, who were the ones that put me to bed just a few hours earlier. But nobody came.

I mustered up the courage to get out of bed and walk to my mom's room. She wasn't there. I walked across the hall to my sister's room. She wasn't there either. I walked down the hallway into the living room and kitchen. Both empty. I walked all the way downstairs to my brother's room. Also, empty. I continued to call out for someone, *anyone,* but nobody answered.

After walking all through the house I slowly ventured out into the garage. Nobody. I continued walking out through the side door and suddenly noticed it was dark. Keeping my hand on the wall of the garage, I walked back toward the doghouse. There, I found Gypsy, our salt and pepper colored German Shepherd laying in a pile of hay. Her smell was familiar, and it made me feel safe. I crawled into the doghouse and curled up next to her. I looked up and noticed a picture of a horse hung squarely over the door. Nice touch, I thought.

I must have fallen asleep because the bright car lights and panicked screams startled me. Gypsy awoke first and slumbered out of the doghouse. I was alone again. And scared. I heard the shouting of my name, "Diane! Diane!" The commotion was loud and overwhelming. I lay there, groggy and confused. Where was I? Why does it smell like this?

I realized that I was in a doghouse and my family was shouting for me. I nestled into the hay and thought, this will teach them a lesson. They had no idea where I was, and I was glad. To hell with them, I thought. I could make this work. I remember thinking at the time, this little doghouse is going to be just fine for me and Gypsy.

I could hear the panic in their voices, but I was not in a hurry to show myself. Let them suffer, I thought. I wanted them to suffer and to feel the way I felt when I was scared.

Eventually, after what seemed like hours, I crawled out of the doghouse and was quickly reunited with my mother. She was appalled at the situation. It was the only time I ever remember my mother, clearly distraught, *truly* yelling at my brother and sister.

As it turns out, ice cream was to blame. My brother and sister put me to bed and went for ice cream. They couldn't have predicted I'd wake up screaming for them. And being kids themselves, it's hard to put off an ice cream craving. It's unfortunate for them that they returned about the same time my mother was pulling into the driveway, or they might have gotten away with the whole thing. It's good to know someone went into my room to check on me; otherwise, I may have spent the entire night in the doghouse. Which, to be honest, would have suited me just fine.

6
Basement Noise

As my brother and sister got older, they took on interests of their own. They grew more independent and ventured out into the world without me. For reasons I didn't understand at the time, they didn't like having me around nearly as much as I wanted to be around them.

My brother founded a hard rock band, called Basement Noise, and it accentuated both the character and dysfunction of our house. He was the drummer, and the youngest of four members. They had regular jam sessions in our basement. As such, AC/DC and Def Leopard rocked the entire house all of the time. Mom approved the idea of hosting Basement Noise because it was her philosophy that she would at least know where her son was and what he was doing. It also meant that it brought a series of motley crew members into our already chaotic house.

We lived in a ranch style house, so the basement was long and wide. A wall divided the space in half, lengthwise, creating two distinct spaces. The band set up a nice little concert venue for themselves in the front half of the basement. As soon as you walked down the stairs, you were greeted by a couch and some chairs for their audience, or, as our judgmental neighbors would say, stoners and hooligans. A dartboard hung on the post in front of the open stairs, making it important to announce yourself as you descended into the space so as to not get stabbed with a flying dart. Their stage filled the back half of the space. They had an impressive amount of equipment for a basement band, including a five-piece drum set, electric guitars, speakers, microphones, tambourines, and an electric keyboard. And behind their stage was a separate space, which was my brother's bedroom.

The other half of the basement housed some homemade storage shelves, a large workbench, where my brother spent hours soldering electrical components for his music equipment, a makeshift shower with just a front curtain for privacy, which was clearly an afterthought, and a laundry area with a chute that allowed you to conveniently drop clothes from the top floor into the basement.

It was an unfinished basement enclosed entirely in concrete, with the exception of the exposed wooden ceiling rafters. Live wires often hung down from those rafters a little farther than a building code might allow. The concrete didn't help with the acoustics at all. In fact, there was really nowhere for the jarring sounds to go but up, out of the house, and into the neighbors' living room.

When they were jamming hard, there was no escaping the noise. Even when the police arrived. First came the doorbell. Then the dogs barking. Followed by loud shouting about who was going to do what. Someone inevitably ran down to the basement screaming for the band to stop. Not understanding the gravity of the situation, they yelled back to leave them alone. And only after the police demanded to speak with an adult did my brother reluctantly come out of the basement to address the situation. But not before a handful of people snuck out the back door.

It's not lost on me, that the outcomes of these situations vary depending on where you live and how you look, but I'd like to think that when a ten-year-old girl wearing footie pajamas and eating a bowl of ice cream opens the door, the knocker might find a soft spot in their heart to at least hear her out.

*

Meanwhile, my sister and Sheila set up shop on the floor in front of the living room television set, playing cards, Scrabble, or Monopoly. They sat inches away from the TV with the volume turned up as loud as it would go, competing with the rock music blaring in the background.

They had stopped trying to put me to bed on time because falling asleep to that kind of noise was impossible. Even if I were deaf, the vibrations alone were enough to keep me awake.

I was pretty lonely most of the time because kids my age weren't allowed over on a regular basis, for some fairly obvious reasons. My best friend, Deanna, who I met years earlier in pre-school, was my mainstay guest. It's likely her mom didn't really understand what was happening around our house; or rather, being a single mom herself, she needed a break so badly that she was willing to overlook it all. So, when Deanna was over, we would get pizza delivered, and sit on the steps watching Basement Noise. The band was pretty good actually.

But when we got bored with the whole thing, we'd sneak out of the house and lay in the backyard, pretending to be at an outdoor concert. Sometimes, if we felt like exploring, we would take off out into the neighborhood.

I lived on a long, dark, country road so the only light came from the houses themselves. On those kind of nights Deanna and I walked through the yards, said hello to the tightly chained neighbor's dog, which always made me sad, and pushed our way through a wall of pine trees just to see what was on the other side. We had all kind of adventures exploring the area at night. If we could find a flashlight laying around the house, we would use it. Otherwise, we just tooled around in the dark. Fortunately, the music was so loud that we never got lost. We just followed the trail of Highway to Hell all the way home.

*

One night, I attempted to talk with my brother during one of the band's intermissions. I must have needed something or was simply bored. So, I went downstairs and knocked on his bedroom door. He didn't answer. I could hear them inside, whispering. I could smell the pot smoke from the other side of the door. And even if I had no sense of smell, I could see it coming from underneath the door. I started banging on the door, hollering, "Let me in!"

Still no answer. Something fiery stirred inside of me, reminding me of all the times that I felt all the things. I mean, how dare you ignore me? I have every right to be in there right now, I thought.

I retreated back to the staircase and stood under the dart board for a moment of stillness, in order to collect all the energy my little body could muster up. I took off in a full sprint like I was at the Olympics and the starter gun went off. As I got close to the door, I leaped up and cannonballed right through the door, smashing it wide open. It flung open and slammed into the wall, bouncing back so quickly it virtually closed itself. My momentum continued to carry me through the doorway, several feet in the air, finally landing me squarely in the center of the room. The stoned bodies made weak attempts to hide their drugs. Shocked myself, I got up, turned toward the partially closed door, and walked out. My brother ran out after me, "What the hell?" he shouted. "What do you want?" he asked.

For the life of me, I had no idea. Nothing. Somehow during my aggressive outburst, I had completely forgotten what I wanted to say to him in the first place.

Bored with the whole thing, and to my brother's complete surprise, I turned and walked back upstairs to see what my sister was doing.

*

Overall, living with a mediocre house band wasn't all bad. One Friday night around my 13th birthday, I invited friends from school over to hang out. Basement Noise was jamming out pretty hard. Between the strobe light and the cigarette smoke, it was quite the show. They were even showing off a little. My brother twirled his drumsticks in the air and the guitar player tucked his lit cigarette into a few of his guitar strings, taking it out every now and then for a puff. I looked around at my friends dancing like they were at a concert. I could see it in their eyes, their brains trying to make sense of it all. Did you *hire* this band for *us*? Or do you actually *live* like this?

They were mesmerized with the show, asking me a million times if this happened all the time.

"Yes," I said. "Yes, it does."

7
Hell No!

My life changed in 3rd grade. Up until that point I ran wild and most people either got out of my way or ignored it completely. A relative once described me as a 'Mack Truck'. I suppose that was true. I was driven by a motor. I went everywhere. And if something was in my way, I just plowed right through it.

I remember short trips to the mall with my mother. Most folks go to the mall for shopping. I saw it as an opportunity to perfect my baseball slide. I would run ahead of her and then suddenly drop hard to the floor and lean into a full-on baseball slide. Over and over, I did this. Store front after store front. From one escalator to the next. And if she was brave enough to take me into a store, I mostly just ran through the clothes racks or accidentally knocked things over. "You're like a bull in a China closet," she said as she escorted me out of the store.

As a kid, if I wanted something to eat, I just ate it. If I wanted to go outside, I just went outside. If I wanted to wear the same Incredible Hulk T-shirt, day after day, I just did. If I didn't want to go to bed, I didn't. This list is long, which is why everything changed in 3rd grade when my teacher told me 'No'.

I had never heard that word before. Well, I heard it, but it never occurred to me actually heed the command. I didn't even really understand what 'no' meant. Like did it mean when I wanted to run as fast as I could in the mall and show the whole world how amazing my baseball slide was that I couldn't? That I had to just *walk*? Like one foot in front of the other? And do *what*? Look at clothes hanging on a hanger? I mean, what kind of world is that for a kid?

So, when my 3rd grade teacher insisted that I follow her directions, I absolutely lost my shit. She told me no when I got out of my chair, walked across the room, and hit another student. She called it violent. I called it trying to make a friend. She told me no when I tilted back in in my chair, balancing on two metal legs. I held the position, folded my arms and glared at her, just to make my point.

I rarely made it outside for recess. It seemed like I was always nose against the wall in the hallway. Which is interesting if you think about it. Eliminating recess for a hyperactive kid makes a terrible afternoon for everyone.

It was rare, but when I did go to recess, I made sure to make contact with every person out there. It was like letting a one-year-old Labrador Retriever out of the crate after an 8-hour workday. I was a stocky, hyper mess desperate for other's affection. I pushed and shoved my way into their friendship circles. Literally, I shoved them all into the ground until they promised to be my friend.

That's when the phone calls home started.

"She is a bully on the playground," the teacher said to my mom.

A few days later, "She literally punched a kid in the gut today. And she tackles everyone on the playground," my teacher said to her exasperated.

"They are all wusses," I told my mom. "I just wanted to play football," I continued, "I don't know how he got the black eye," I lied.

These things went on for the next few years in school, resulting in after school tutors and referrals for counseling. The tutoring was effective because it gave me a chance to have some alone time with my teachers, giving them the chance to see how incredibly funny I could be when not otherwise shut down by mundane classroom rules. The referrals for counseling, on the other hand, seemed to evaporate upon entry into my home environment.

In 5th grade, I got a little more daring with my behavior. "Let's go hide behind the garbage cans and watch the bus go by," I said to my neighbor one morning before school. She was caught off guard by the idea but seemed up for the adventure. As we saw the bus approach from the distance, we bolted across the street toward the garbage cans next to her house. We ducked down real low and waited. I peeked over the can and saw the bus put its lights on, slow to a stop, wait a minute, then roll off.

I popped up from behind the cans and started walking toward my house. "That was fun," I said laughing.

"What do we do *now*?" she asked.

I had no idea what we should do, but I had the house to myself for the whole day and I couldn't have been more excited about it.

A little while later, when I just settled in for a snack and some TV, my neighbor sheepishly knocked on my door.

"Hey," I said standing in the doorway.

"So, um, yea, my mom is taking me to school and, um, I'm supposed to ask if you want a ride too," she said.

I thought about it for a moment. Looked around the house. Took it all in. "No, I'm fine," I said. And closed the door.

I got grounded for a week after that one.

A little while after the garbage can incident, I got kicked off the bus entirely. During one particularly rough day, I swiftly moved through the spectrum of discipline cards — warning, yellow, blue. And then finally, she had enough. Red. I was suspended from the bus for a week. The incident leading up to the final straw wasn't my fault, entirely. I can't recall the details, and who said what first, but I'm sure there was a very good reason why I took a running leap over three seats like Evil Knievel while she was driving 40 MPH down the road.

My mom got a lot of phone calls from the school, but she was at a complete loss about the whole bus situation. She knew she couldn't transport me to and from school because of her exhausting work schedule, so out of desperation, she invited the bus driver over for dinner one night. There's nothing like having the bus driver you antagonize on a daily basis ring the doorbell to your house. My mom insisted that I open the door, greet her, and invite her in for dinner.

The three of us sat around the table for what seemed like hours. Carrie. I remember her name. I heard all about her life and pets. No kids, which surprised me. She was a real nice lady. After that dinner, something clicked inside of my head. I saw her as a *person*, not just some bus driver whose job it was to take me to school. That realization drastically changed my bus behavior. Not only were there no more suspensions, but I nominated myself to become the official bus monitor. Overnight, it was my job to keep everyone's behavior in check, which, as it turns out, I was pretty good at.

*

Fifth grade was also the year I finally got glasses. I find it interesting that, while they publicly weighed us every year, they completely missed my poor vision.

If you don't know what public weighing is, it's when your entire class goes out into the hallway, lines up against the wall, and waits patiently to get weighed on a scale centered in the middle of the hall.

To be clear, lining up 30 plus eleven-year-olds in alphabetical order in a short time period can be quite challenging. Fortunately, it was a drill that we practiced regularly. I knew exactly who was supposed to be standing in front of, and behind me. Of course, challenges arose if someone was absent; but mostly, we had it down to a science.

*

I imagine that if the teacher officially declared it the Day of Public Weighing, and announced the event to the entire class, I might have feigned ill, faked an injury, or created such a distraction she would have no choice but to cancel the event.

I could have juggled glue sticks; or even better, *ate* the glue sticks, which would have given me a pass straight to the clinic. I could have accidentally jammed a few fingers into the pencil sharpener, poked my own eye out with a spitball, or just set the scale on fire.

But she didn't announce the reason behind lining up. We didn't even have a chance to prepare for the event. I might have at least *tried* to lose a few pounds. Maybe. But probably not.

The Day of Public Weighing was the worst day of the year. Particularly for us chubby kids. The practice was new to middle school, and the whole thing felt like a circus. Some administrator, or ring master, made the decision to measure each student's height and weight once a year and include that information on the final report card. So not only was a student evaluated on their academic performance and conduct, but also their apparent height and weight trends.

Around that time, without any real knowledge or structure to my dietary habits, I pretty much shoveled into my face whatever looked good and was readily available. "Don't eat that, you'll spoil your dinner," was not a thing I heard growing up.

"Stop shoving cookies into your mouth," or "Save some for the rest of us," sounded more familiar.

To be fair, I got a lot of pressure to not waste food. One time my dad took me to Perkins for breakfast. It was kind of a big deal for us because we didn't eat out that much. Perkins was pretty fancy for us back then. I looked through the menu and was immediately mesmerized by the dessert-looking stack of pancakes. I passed over all the healthy choices and zoomed in on the picture with the giant stack of pancakes, topped with strawberry fruit syrup and whip cream. "This," I said to the waitress, pointing with my chubby finger.

My dad tried to talk me out of it. "That looks too sweet, kid," he said.

"That's what I want," I said firmly. He didn't push back.

A little while later the pancakes came out and they were practically stacked as high as my forehead. I immediately poured syrup all over them.

I took about three bites and shoved the plate back. "It's too sweet," I said.

"Oh, it's too sweet, huh?" my dad said back to me in his

best 10-year-old, spoiled girl voice.

"I can't eat these," I cried.

My dad pushed the plate back in front of me and said, "Oh, you're going to eat these if we have to sit here all day."

"Well, I don't have anywhere to be, so…" I replied.

My dad's nostrils flared, and he began eating his eggs and bacon, and I stared quietly at the mound of sugar in front of me.

I slowly cut into my breakfast, tears running down my face, forcing my mouth to open. Each bite seemed to triple in sweetness and size as it hit my stomach, like someone was pumping sugary air into each pancake morsel. My stomach expanded like a balloon that was about to pop. My brother and sister were there and did what they could to help. But it all seemed so insurmountable. I finished the pancakes the best I could, and we eventually did leave the restaurant. I was sick the rest of the day.

I'm not saying he wasn't right to hold me accountable for my frivolous order, but I'm wondering if that was the situation to make a point — forcing me to eat a 2,000-plus calorie breakfast when I was already marching towards childhood obesity.

It's fair to say that I grew up in a house where portion control, or serving sizes, were recommended on a formula largely determined by what was available or who might beat you to the thing. No hot dogs meant a TV dinner and some chocolate chip cookies. No TV dinners meant canned spaghetti-O's with frozen French fries, a substitute for boxed macaroni and cheese. No chocolate chip cookies meant a few clicks of Cheez Whiz shot directly into your mouth, for dessert. It's all pretty straight forward really.

I was an active kid though, always getting into this or that. Running here or there. So, mathematically, it didn't make sense for me, to be as chubby as I was. But alas, I was full faced, double chinned, rounded belly, and enlarged thighs chubby.

To be honest, I didn't have a complex about it. I never really cared in the way most people care. I wasn't flaunting it, by any means, running through the halls singing "Look at me, ooh-la-la — Chubby Wubby is here."

But I wasn't hiding in bathrooms either.

I say all of that to say, the whole getting weighed in front of people was a bit too much.

We were marched to the main hallway like trained animals in a circus. Our classroom teacher, and circus trainer, Ms. Bella, took pride in her control, waving her clipboard at us like a whip. She leaned in close to make a point, then backed out to give us space; to signify she trusted us, and we could, in turn, trust her. She turned corners sharply, standing at the angle so she could see us both come and go. It was a brilliant tactic.

A tall, steel, physician's scale stood center stage. The florescent lights beamed down on the shiny metal frame, making it impossible to miss. I saw it as soon as I turned the corner. The bastard. It mocked me and I was pissed. It felt like a magnetic force was pulling me closer while I desperately thought of ways to escape, not ruling anything out.

I could just run. Jump ship entirely. Leave the building screaming, "To hell with you all!" I could smack other kids in the face to wake them from the body shaming culture we were conditioned to buy into. I could lunge at the trainer, rip the clipboard out of her claws, and devour it for good measure. The clipboard. It controlled us. Eliminating it removes her power, I thought.

But I did none of those things.

"Hug the wall tight and don't get out of order," the trainer commanded. "This is very important," she continued.

I complied.

"Remain silent and stay still," we heard. Two things virtually impossible for middle schoolers.

But the clipboard. It had a hold of us.

I stood in the long thin line against the wall like a plump tomato on a plate of string beans.

The announcer, or nurse, eagerly awaited our arrival. She proudly stood center stage, next to her beloved scale. Her white hat sat squarely on her pale, expressionless face, which matched her coat. She firmly held a yard stick, a sign of preparedness.

Our trainer, feeling confident in her pack, moved to join the announcer. The magnetic force multiplied.

The first name was called. Dutifully, the girl stepped up onto the scale and was still.

"Nine-ty-Fi-ive!" the announcer shouted with flair. The number echoed down the silenced hallway.

And the crowed silently awed. Is this good? Bad? What does this even mean? Twisting their fingers and holding their breath, they eagerly awaited the next name.

Having the last name beginning with 'R', I witnessed this routine far too long before hearing my very own wretched number echo through the hallway.

It's like my number became a riff hammered out by an electric bass player. It took on a life of its own. It was shocking, hard on the ears, and completely unavoidable. It commanded the attention of the audience in a way that mesmerized them.

It seemed like the show-stopping riff hit every locker, doorknob, and light fixture before finally resting on the last soft corner of an empty classroom.

I'm sure the practice of public weighing started with good intentions. Perhaps it fell under the umbrella of health education or a way to monitor the overall health of students. But behind the scenes, it became a spectacle of public shaming for students who fell outside the norm.

Over time, I gained the courage to ask that my number be whispered to the record keeper. It led to others asking that their number also be whispered. After a few years of this spectacle, the whole thing mysteriously went away altogether.

*

Many years later, while struggling my way through college, I discovered that I was almost deaf in one ear. "I'm surprised your speech is as good as it is given your significant hearing loss," the audiologist said after the examination.

Having been an emotionally unregulated and overweight kid with poor vision and hearing caused me, and others, a great deal of grief growing up. But it also led me to a career dedicated to helping similar kinds of kids. Kids fighting uphill battles. Marching to the beats of their own drum. Navigating all kind of situations. Or the kinds of kids who push through a wall of pine trees just to see what's on the other side.

*

After years of being a teacher for emotionally challenged students and now, a school psychologist, I can confidently diagnose the earlier version of myself. What I had going on in those early years was a combination of ADHD and sensory integration issues (to have my socks on perfect or temper tantrums would ensue, all of my tags needed to be cut out of my clothes, and the constant seeking out intense sensory experiences like pushing and tackling). Add to all of that, some vision and hearing issues, and a generalized aversion to the word NO.

That's a lot for a kid to manage all at one time, especially during a time when my parents were otherwise distracted, and teachers were not entirely trained on such things.

*

Some good did come out of all the behavior issues though. I felt more connected with school staff. I was in the principal's office so much I could name every person in her framed family photo. They gave me so many odd jobs around the school, I pretty much had run of the halls and spent quality time with the custodians, lunch ladies, and office staff. I've been slow to get to this point, because I feel it's fairly obvious, but I was a funny kid. It's true that I was a hot mess in so many other ways. But I was funny; a real jokester. I kept the class laughing as much as I could, anything to distract from doing work.

A few teachers did get it right, and those were the ones I worked for. A few were so far off that I couldn't help but show them every day how terrible they were. One teacher, in particular, got so frustrated with me one day that I remember her vehemently scolding me as she stuck her crooked middle finger in my face. I couldn't get over how crooked her finger was, why she was using her middle finger to point, how she could possibly live with all of that chalk dust on her finger, and why she smelled like coffee and rotten eggs. Anyway, I can't remember what she said, but I do vaguely remember my reaction to her caused quite a stir, followed by her marching me down to the principal's office.

The office ladies really liked me, so they greeted me with a smile. "Hi Diane!" one said smiling. And that just got my teacher even more mad. She was yelling about this or that and the office lady just smiled and told me to have a seat. They were so nice about the whole thing. My teacher paced back and forth, waiting for the principal to see us. Having no luck, she left in a huff.

I felt comfortable in the office. It was a busy place, so I got to see everybody — teachers, students, parents, delivery guys. I helped fold papers, stuff envelopes, whatever they needed. It became my alternative during school assemblies too. That happened after I stood up and shouted something at the guest speaker one time. To be fair, I thought it was meant to be an interactive event and that we lived in a country with free speech. So, instead of going to assemblies, I just went to the office. It just seemed to be better for everyone. It speaks to the importance of school culture as a whole, though, in that a student can feel connected where you least expect it. And it's not always *in* the classroom.

8
On Building Courage

As a School Psychologist, parents often ask me how they can build confidence in their kids; how they can make them more resilient and able to handle challenging situations.

I find this to be one of the most challenging questions because the answer is complicated. To a large degree, it depends on the nature of your child and the level of risk you're willing to take as a parent. Some fear is healthy and overcoming that to achieve a goal is powerful and builds confidence when faced with future challenges. But too much fear can be debilitating, and if pushed too hard, can create increased anxiety and possibly lasting trauma. And the line between the two can be ever so slight.

Failure is possible, if not probable. However, it's less about failing and more about how we move through it. It's easy to get stuck when you can't step back to see the bigger picture. I call it wearing blinders.

Blinders are put on horses so they don't get distracted with everything going on around them. Which makes sense for the horses because, in theory, it allows them to perform better. But wearing blinders prevents you from gaining full understanding of a situation. And, well, we're not horses. We're humans who need to understand the full scope of what's going on around us in order to effectively make good choices that will enable us to be more successful.

I try to tell the students I work with that using a variety of strategies and thinking flexibly about a problem will likely lead to a more successful outcome. And I try to tell parents that teaching children how to remove the blinders early in their development will likely pad their future falls; whereby, small failures hurt a lot less and can even help them bounce right back up.

When you're able to step back and see the bigger picture, you're likely to realize that they're not failures at all. They're just missteps that can be corrected, leading to a more favorable outcome and stronger sense of self.

Since I don't have children, I rely heavily on my own experiences as a kid and what worked or didn't work. I try to marry that with the present-day version of myself and our current culture, and offer up an answer that is relevant, insightful, and not too scary.

For example, I can't say to parents, "Just throw them in the water and they will learn to swim."

I would be fired.

But if you asked me, how did you learn to be courageous and resilient?

I would begin with the fact that growing up free-range lends itself to plenty of opportunities to make mistakes. I didn't always have someone standing over me, telling me how to do something; let alone, do it for me. As a result, I learned a lot of hard lessons trying to get something right. I don't know if courage and resilience was something I was taught, or that it's something that already lived inside of me and just needed nurtured, or some combination of both. But ultimately, I learned how to work a problem, dig deep, and move through challenging situations. Two childhood stories, in particular, stand out as examples.

*

One time my dad took me camping with his buddies and their kids. A lot of my stories start off this way. He loaded all of our bikes up on the back of his van and, as we drove through the hills of Pennsylvania, we embarked on this enormous hill.

"This is the hill that destroys the brakes, kid, especially with the boat or a lot of gear," he said.

I mean this hill was awesome. So awesome that when we were climbing it, I said that I thought it would be fun to ride my bike down. He clung onto that statement like it was doctrine.

"You got it kid," he said with crazy eyes.

An hour after we set up camp we were back at the top of the hill. He unloaded three bikes. Mine, and the two belonging to his buddy's sons. One of them was already crying. I could feel my stomach start to turn while he was checking the tires and chain on my bike. I looked over and both boys were crying. My dad looked down at me, as if to say, don't even think about it.

He must have sensed my fear because he leaned in hard, "This was your idea, kid. You'll be fine. Just hold those handlebars real tight. Man, you are going to fly!" he screamed.

This was all before bike helmets were a thing. So, it was just me and my cut off jean shorts, low top tennis shoes, and my favorite Incredible Hulk T-shirt. I touched my chest. I figured, if the Hulk can do it, so can I.

We were all standing on the side of the road, and before I

even took off, the boys were already trying to crawl back into the car without him seeing. But my dad made them go back to their bikes. For me, there was no going back. He was right. It was my idea.

"Ok, I'll follow behind you guys and see you at the bottom!" he screamed as he got back into the car.

I started rolling and I remembered his words, 'just hold those handlebars real tight.' I must have only pedaled a few seconds before I felt the wind blowing in my face. I picked up speed quickly. I held my breath and just kept going faster and faster. I feathered my pedal brakes the best I could, but it was hard to coordinate my hands and feet at such a fast rate of speed.

Man, I was FLYING! Drool was coming out of my mouth. My hair was in and out of my eyes, and the bugs were hitting me hard in the face. I wanted to look back to see if he was still there like he said he would be. But I was paralyzed in the downhill position, eyes wide open and staring ahead.

After several minutes the hill leveled off before a steeper decline around the bend. I managed to slow down and pull off long enough to look behind me and see my dad loading the boys' bikes into the station wagon in the middle of the first hill. He was way back there.

I decided to wait for him. When he finally rolled up, I could see the boys huddled together in the back seat. He leaned out his window. "What's the matter?" he asked looking sternly at me. His eyes scanned my bike.

"Nothing," I said. "I just saw you load their bikes up and—"

"Yea, you're good, kid. This is the best part of the hill right here!" he said enthusiastically. "I'm right behind you," he said.

The conversation was over.

Off I went and I don't know how I managed to hold on and keep the bike upright for the next several miles, but I did. And he was right. It was pretty awesome. That last leg was the best part of the hill.

I still ride to this day, and I still love a good hill. And I always hold onto the handlebars real tight.

*

As a kid, if I wasn't on a bike, I was in the water.

Water is like royalty to my father. And he is the King. If I was walking upright independently, I was also swimming. Despite my mother's pleas, he put me in the water as soon as he felt it was reasonably safe to do so. To be clear, his judgment on this matter is questionable, and 'safe' tends to be subjective in my family.

I was waterskiing when most kids were learning to tie their shoes. My dad put a lifejacket on me and threw me in the water, put two water skis on my little feet, handed me a handle attached to a long rope, and told me to hold on tight.

"It's just like getting out of a chair," he shouted.

I sat in the water holding onto this handle, unsure of what was going to happen. My hands barely fit around the thing.

"Keep the tips up!" he shouted from the boat.

I kept my tips up.

He slowly pulled me through the water, and I could feel the resistance. I held on to the handle as tight as I could and let the water do its job. I could feel it want to push me up, so I let it.

"When you're ready, just yell 'Hit it'!" he shouted.

I felt it so I yelled as loud as I could, "Hit It!"

He accelerated and the handle tried to leave me, but I held on hard. I immediately lost my tips and the handle turned into a cannonball that I was trying to hold onto, but then my skis fell off and my legs fell behind me. I held on like he said, taking in water like a sunken ship. I couldn't see. I couldn't breathe. It was me and that handle to the end, I thought.

After several minutes it all stopped. I popped up out of the water, coughing, still holding onto the handle, and he was right next to me. Sitting in the boat.

"Ok kid. Listen, that's my fault," he said leaning over the side.

I looked up at him, "What?"

"I forgot to tell you to let go of the handle if it wasn't going to happen," he said apologetically.

I could let go? It never occurred to me to let go. I didn't even know that was an option.

Over and over, he pulled me, and I fell. Sometimes he would tell me to take a break, "let someone else go out, you can try again later."

Eventually I did get up. But only after a few hundred failed attempts. And this is true for most successful water skiers because rarely does anyone get up on their first try.

*

As the years went on, he threw new challenges at us on the regular. "Try dropping one ski!" he would shout from the boat. "One hand it!" he would scream. "Who wants take off from the dock?" he asked with crazy eyes.

"Let's get both you and your sister out there," he said one

74

day. And he pulled me and my sister up together. "Ok, now let's get all three of you up at the same time," he said. My brother jumped in with us. And we all three got up. That last one was a highlight for him, for sure. In one pull, he got all three of his kids up on skis. We managed to hold on for a while too. And there is a picture to prove it.

He was generous with my friends, taking them out and teaching them how to ski. He was far more patient with them than he ever was with us. He didn't make any of them cry. There's someone reading this story now saying, "Yea, your dad taught me how to water ski and it was a blast!"

When giving lessons got boring, he added new water toys. "Here, try this kneeboard. I have no idea how it works," he said throwing it out to me.

And the inner tube. It was a giant black rubber inner tube off a large truck tire. He picked it up at the junk yard one day. It had a needle the size of a four-inch knife and his only instruction was to, "Hold on to the tube real tight and don't let that needle stab you in the gut."

Nowadays I see kids out riding on all sorts of floatable toys. They sure look all safe and comfortable on them. In fact, they look like proper flotation devices. It always makes me chuckle and I just think, you have no idea...

Tubing became a cult. It was a rite of passage. The more kids on it the better. The faster the better. The crazier the turns, the better. He took great joy in trying to throw us off the damn thing. Laughing hysterically when he succeeded.

*

And when he got bored with our regular lake, he took us on

adventures to explore new lakes. One time he loaded us all up and took us to a lake in West Virginia, called Tiger Lake. It started off like any other camping/boating trip, where we set up the tent and cots, fought over who was going to sleep where, and who was going to do what chore.

We finally got down to the lake and backed the boat into the water. We were all standing in the water holding the boat when my sister saw it first. A black water snake. She screamed and hurried back onto shore. I ran up after her, leaving my brother to hold the boat by himself. That's when we saw all of them. Everywhere. Black water snakes zipping around the shallow water, in and out of rocks, under the dock, and back around to the shoreline.

My dad took to investigating the water snake situation, and realizing things were about to blow up quickly, shouted from the dock, "These things only like shallow water! They don't like the deeper water, where we'll be… and they're not going to hurt you anyway!"

Not having much experience with such things and taking him for his word that water snakes didn't like deep water, we all jumped into the boat and off we went.

My brother went out first. He skied around the lake and finally dropped off. Next, it was my sister's turn, who adamantly refused to leave the safety of her seat. Clearly not trusting my father's knowledge on the habits of water snakes, she remained steadfast in her seated position.

After what seemed like a lifetime of cajoling, he got a life jacket on her and had her sitting on the edge of the boat. He had her on the edge of the boat because there wasn't a ladder to get in and out of the water. As a result, we were forced to climb over the edge and abruptly drop into the water. The only thing worse than this, was trying to climb back into the damn thing when you were waterlogged and numb from being yanked all around the lake. Short on patience, it usually meant that my dad just grabbed you by the bottom of your life jacket and violently hoisted you up and over the edge, forcing you to land hard on the floor of the boat.

He managed to sweet talk her enough to crawl over the edge, but she refused to put her feet in the water. My sister, who was a tall and lanky pre-teen, used what appeared to be super-human core strength to grasp the edge of the boat with her hands while also keeping her legs completely out of the water. Before our eyes, she slowly morphed her body into something like a Stretch Armstrong as she then brought her feet back up to the edge, meeting her tightly clenched hands.

It was quite the spectacle. Even my dad was speechless. But it didn't stop him from gently tapping her hands in an effort to get her to release her grip. I watched in horror from the back seat, as he tapped each of her limbs until she could no longer hold on. SPLASH!

This was immediately followed by a series of shrieking sounds, not unlike a fox's mating call. It sounded like someone was being murdered.

He quickly threw a ski out to her and put the motor in gear. To the surprise of no one, she got up on the first try and off we went.

As soon as she dropped off, the shrieking started all over again. She was flailing around in the water like a shark was attacking her. My dad quickly pulled the boat around and without any assistance whatsoever, my sister shot out of the water like a rocket and threw herself back into the boat. With long black hair, she looked like a drowned rat when she came in. She was exhausted. And pissed.

Shortly after that scene unfolded, "Well, kid, you're up," my dad said unapologetically. "We came all this way so we're all going to make a go of it."

Having watched my sister's horrific experience, and seeing the look in my dad's eyes, I was determined to just get it over with. I put my life jacket on and jumped in. My dad bent down and rose up holding one ski. He threw it out to me, and it skidded beautifully across the water into my hands. I put it on. And waited for the second ski.

Nothing.

I watched him move back to the helm and put the engine in gear.

"Hey!" I shouted. "Give me the other ski!"

"Today is the day, kid!" he shouted. "You're going to learn to slalom ski!"

I sat all by myself in the water about sixty feet behind the boat. Waiting. Keeping my tip up. Wondering if my dad was a monster.

Just before I felt the tension, a black water snake wrapped itself around the rubber binding, inches away from my ankle. I screamed so loud and then, VROOM! He took off, but I couldn't hold on and lost the handle. I just kept screaming. "Hurry! Hurry!"

He came back around and told me to try again. He was shouting out instructions from the boat. It seemed so far away. *HE* seemed so far away. Snakes were swimming around me. I knew it.

"Find your balance!" He shouted. Then, "Crouch, but not too much! You can keep a foot in. Or not. Whatever is comfortable! But don't get too comfortable!" he shouted.

The pressure was all too much.

He pulled me again. And again, I lost the handle. We did this a handful more times until, finally, I popped up out of the water, on one ski. He didn't zip me around like usual. He just kept a nice, steady, straight pace. I could vaguely see him, holding onto the steering wheel with one hand, and cheering me on with the other. He was hollering something at me, and then I fell.

That wrapped up our afternoon, and it was a quiet night around the campsite, for some fairly obvious reasons. My sister stayed pissed. For days. Probably even years.

*

During these waterskiing adventures, the falls were hard and frequent. When he pulled the boat around, we were always greeted with a, "You look good out there, kid." Even though we all looked like wet rag dolls with potential internal injuries.

And no matter how tired you were, if you asked to come in, he'd say, "Just relax out there... float for a while." And he'd shut the boat off, grab a bag of potato chips, sit on the back of the boat, and tell you a long story about something obscure. His stories always ended with, "Ready for another run?"

One fall, in particular, was memorable. I was cruising along on one ski. Somehow the inner tube came loose from the back of the boat, and before I knew it, I was completely airborne. I did a few summersaults in the air and then face planted hard in the water. I lay there laughing because I literally thought I was dead. I remember seeing the back of the boat still moving forward. He doesn't see me, I thought. He doesn't know I fell.

I bobbed up and down in the water for several minutes taking stock of my limbs and faculties. Can I feel my legs? Yes. My hands? Yes. Do you know where you are? Yes. I had no idea where my ski was though. Finally, he came back around.

I told him everything that happened.

"Sorry, kid. We missed it," he said matter of factly. He was so distracted talking to Deanna that neither of them witnessed the most magnificent fall of my life. My ski was a good 50 yards away.

"Well, come on in and get some grapes," he said.

Grapes.

*

I can't say that my father's approach to building courage and resiliency in his kids is the best approach, but it made sense to him at the time. And arguably, it worked.

Years later I asked him about that ski trip and the snakes.

"I knew you were pretty motivated to get up because of the snakes," he said. "Christ, who wouldn't be? They were everywhere," he added.

"And lying about them only liking the shore?"

"Well, what was I supposed to do?" he asked. "Just pack up and go home?"

That was the extent of his thought process.

He certainly didn't intend to traumatize us or anything. In fact, he was just as surprised as we were about the water snakes. Moreover, I'm sure he envisioned a much more enjoyable trip that what actually occurred. But he's not a guy that walks away from a challenging situation. On the contrary, he usually doubles down on the thing. And if there's one thing about my dad, he expects you to do the same.

Would I have preferred a softer approach? A gentler method of parenting? Of course. But I had what I had at the time, and I just needed to figure it all out or I was going to miss a lot of potentially fun opportunities. I had to use the tools I had in my back pocket. A sense of humor. A willingness to try new things. And, I learned over the years to listen to *what* he said and not necessarily *how* he said it.

If I sat around with blinders on, or let fear of the unknown fester, I might not have ever gotten on the bike, or learned to slalom ski. Which would have been fine also, by the way. Because those sorts of things aren't for everyone.

But in doing those things; or in doing similar risk-taking kinds of things, I gained a level of confidence that led to other new experiences. And those new experiences led to other new experiences. I learned that if something didn't go right the first time, I could regroup and try it again. And again. And gradually, over time, I learned that I was pretty capable of handling all sorts of interesting situations.

Somewhere in all of this, my dad did more than create memories for us. He turned waterskiing into a series of life lessons. Never give up. Failure is necessary for success. Believe in yourself. Don't be afraid to try new things. Don't walk away from a challenge without at least trying. Don't take a beautiful day for granted. Keep your tips up. And finally, no matter what anyone tells you, snakes *do* like deep water.

9
My Bout with Religion

My free-range childhood ended abruptly when I was fourteen. My mom came home from work one day and told us she was marrying a minister. Nothing screams, 'life as you know it is over,' like an ordained minister. Lazy Sundays mulling around the neighborhood with my friends, stealing ice cream cakes from the Dairy Queen, and sneaking booze into our bedrooms for future parties was soon replaced with church, followed by the church social hour, and Sunday night bible study to round out the day. The sharp contrast of past and present made me dizzy, and it sparked what would become, a deep seated, life-long resentment toward organized religion.

Prior to this announcement, I didn't know anything about church. To be clear, I didn't know anything about church because there wasn't an expectation that I *should* know something about church. I don't recall it ever coming up in conversation. It's not like I would watch my mom wandering around the house on Sunday morning mumbling something about how we should all stop being heathens and start going to church. I don't ever remember her saying, 'Praise God' or 'God Bless' after hearing some good news. I don't even think there was a hard and fast rule about saying 'God bless you' after a sneeze.

In fact, my mom studied astrology for years. Which is the

complete opposite of organized religion. When I was much younger, she belonged to an astrology club, which was a lot like a cult for beginners. I remember being carted off to an old farmhouse where her and some other folks would sit around, studying charts, aspects, and orbits. It teetered on fortune telling really, and after one particularly strange event that she would never talk about, she stopped going to the club. And I stopped seeing my astrology friends.

*

After that incident, my mother became a closet astrologer, secretly reading charts and analyzing orbits and aspects. She was generally unphased by events because she seemed to always know what was about to happen, or that she totally expected the thing to happen, because of how the stars had been aligned.

*

For my whole life, Easter and Christmas came and went without so much as a nod to God or The Church. As far as I knew, Santa Claus and the Easter Bunny were the real deities. I prayed to them for all sorts of things. A new Atari video game. Some marshmallow peeps. Anything I could play or eat.

Up until that point, I may have been in a church once or twice for a wedding. Other kids seemed to know so much more about religion. In the school cafeteria during lunch, I would listen to my friends talk about church and Sunday School. I never really had much to contribute to those kinds of conversations so a lot of times I just made stuff up.

"What are you?" they asked me one time. I really had no idea. What *was* I? I wasn't raised a particular religion, so I drew on my memory of something I read one time about the Jehovah Witnesses celebrating in a Kingdom Hall, and I thought that was pretty cool. So that's what I picked. The Kingdom Hall. It was an impulsive choice, I now realize, and one that almost lost me my Homeroom Birthday Celebration.

I did go to Vacation Bible School with a neighbor one summer, but my competitive nature caused a rift between us, and I was never invited back. Who knew learning the Books of Bible could get a person into so much trouble?

It all started with my seventh-grade English teacher, Mr Lightfoot. He wanted us to learn the helping verbs, and he ran regular competitions for how fast you could say the helping verbs without making any mistakes. Every few days he would ring a bell and all those who wanted to enter the contest would jump up and give it a go. I used to stay up late at night memorizing and practicing them.

Am Are Is Be Been Was Were Have Has Had Do Does Did May Can Must Might Could Would Should Shall Will.

My energy, was to be commended, the teacher told me after I finished. But, alas, I came in second every time. The same kid, Michael, always beat me by a few seconds. I tried to make the case to Mr Lightfoot that Michael blended the words together; that he wasn't, in fact, saying each word in isolation. But the teacher was a stickler for the timer so in the end, Michael was always faster.

So, when I got to Vacation Bible School later that summer, they handed me a list and said we were going to learn the books of the Bible, and I thought with Mike being out of the picture, I was sure to win. Once again, I found myself staying up late each night, memorizing and practicing. Over and over again I practiced the list in my head. I walked around the house like a demonically possessed person preparing for an interview with an underground cult.

Genesis Exodus Numbers Deuteronomy Joshua Judges Ruth First and Second Samuel First and Second Kings First and Second Chronicles Ezra Nehemiah Esther Job Psalms Proverbs Ecclesiastes (though I always pronounced it Ecclesiastics.) Song of Songs Isaiah Jeremiah.

I truly believed the faster I said them, not only would I win, but the closer to God I would become. A dedicated disciple, I thought.

I walked into Vacation Bible School the following morning ready to rock. The teacher started to call off names to go up and recite the books of the Bible. I couldn't believe what a pathetic showcase it was. They were painstakingly slow. I couldn't tell if they were praying or reciting the list. I started wiggling in my seat. Biting my tongue. Rocking back and forth. I wanted to go before I forgot them all. I was growing impatient. Before I knew what happened I jumped up and shouted, "Jesus Christ! It's..." and I rattled off the list with lightning speed. Frantically out of breath I sat down, beaming with pride at my pace. It was clearly faster than everyone else's.

Apparently the "Jesus Christ" part was a showstopper because nobody noticed how fast I recited the list. My excitement also caused me to inadvertently interrupt my neighbor as she wasn't quite finished with her list. I was promptly told that saying, "Jesus Christ" in that context was taking the Lord's name in vain; which to be fair, I did not know. I heard Jesus Christ every day of my life, and not once did I hear someone say afterwards that it's taking the Lord's name in vain. Had I known that I would have led with something else entirely.

I was told I couldn't return to Vacation Bible School unless one of my parents came back with me, which was actually not my first-time hearing that. I heard it at my first, and last, Girl Scout meeting. And also at the Roller Rink, after a very unfortunate turn of events involving an angry floor guard.

In hindsight and having been in education for all of my adult life, I realized a good teacher, or true Christian even, would have turned my youthful energy into a real passion for Jesus Christ, rather than scolding me and sending me away feeling ashamed. It's a lesson that I have always kept in my back pocket when working with kids. You need to actually *teach* the behavior if you want to *expect* the behavior. Also, and this is an important one, channel a kid's energy for the good before it turns evil.

To hell with them, I thought. It was an excellent performance. And I never went back.

The real problem with my mom marrying a minister was not that he was a minister, though that was, inherently, a real problem; but rather, that he was also my uncle. By marriage, of course. As a kid, I ran around on holidays calling him Uncle Rob. He was a pretty fast and loose kind of guy. A real drinker and piece of work. A cocky business guy with questionable associates. He had a near death experience one night, divorced my aunt, and found the Lord. And also, my mom, apparently.

And just like that, she became his third wife. My uncle became my stepdad. My cousin became my stepbrother. And my aunt stopped talking to us altogether. It's all pretty straightforward really.

The Lord found his way into our house like an uninvited guest with lice. A stranger we avoided like the Plague. He was charged with saving an impossible crew. A cowboy trying to wrangle water. He was the new kid at school. Ignored, teased and plotted against. Despite the Lord's best efforts, he met resistance at every corner.

I weaved in and out of his presence like a drunken lunatic, paranoid he would zap me with a magical laser, changing me into a normal kid. A follower, even. I slipped in and out of the house at all hours of the night. Anything to throw him off my scent. When I got bored with avoiding, I started to blame him for various things.

"Why is your room a mess?"

The Lord did it.

"Why are there dishes in the sink?

The Lord said to leave them.

The resentment grew exponentially because a little while after the Lord rolled in, rules started to follow. Dinnertime. Bedtime. No swearing. And suddenly, I had to mind manners that I hadn't quite yet learned. It was brutal and my free-range brain couldn't make sense of the whole thing.

My brother would have no part of it and moved out. My sister immersed herself in all things outside of the home. I still had four years of high school to deal with the nonsense. It was going to be a painful journey with impossible odds.

My mom's new marriage came with a new business and a new house. A real trifecta. It seemed that, overnight, we were upgraded to middle class where food and nicer cars became readily available. As a result, my friendship circle grew, and sports became increasingly more important.

But things began to get weird. They started talking in terms of what the Ministry needed. Donations. A youth group. More donations. Because I was the only teenager in the house, I was called upon to bring my friends over to the house for a Bible study. This was a hard sell because most kids my age were already signed up for one religion or another. And there weren't too many 15-year-olds eager to get invited to a Bible study. I got desperate one day and asked my best friend.

"Fuck that," she said before I could finish the question.

And I asked another, who said she would totally come to a Bible study if we could go out drinking afterwards.

"Sure," I said. "Totally makes sense."

The youth group was a bust. But things continued to get interesting as missionaries from all over the world became regular house guests. One night a pair of non-English speaking gentlemen came to dinner and didn't leave for a month. They cuddled up in our one spare bedroom, sharing a bed, and giggling themselves to sleep each night.

"Lock your door," my sister said to me each night they stayed. "Jesus, they're weird," she finished.

Jesus is right. Everything was about Jesus. Jesus this. Jesus that. Praise Jesus. It was exhausting.

I thought it was weird when one of the missionaries showed up at my bedroom door one night holding a white dove. "I do magic," he told me in his best English. "For Jesus," he said petting the dove.

Of course it's for Jesus, I thought. Everything is for Jesus.

He handed me the dove like it was a precious stone. I didn't want to be rude, so I feigned excitement and accepted it. It's not like I had a cage laying around, or bird food. I just kind of let him walk around my room that night, which was a terrible idea because he shit all over the place. And although his wings were clipped, he fluttered around just enough to keep things interesting.

I kind of grew attached to the thing. I named him Casper. A few days later, the missionary brought me another white dove. And then another. I had no idea where he was getting the doves from because he didn't have a car to drive. And it's not like he packed them in his suitcase and brought them all the way from his home country. Before I knew it, I had a half dozen white doves fluttering around my room.

I had the doves for a while, until they started to outgrow their space and I was ankle deep in their shit. A few died and we eventually re-homed the rest. I secretly wanted to be re-homed with them because, much like the dove shit, the religious chatter was piling up all around me. I could barely breathe.

I was guilted into going to church regularly, which was incredibly annoying. At one point, I tried to buy into it. I really did. I sat in the hard church pew watching the worshippers. Gauging their level of commitment. To the church. To God. To each other. One time I was snapped out of my own thoughts by this weird sound to my right. The lady sitting next to me started mumbling in a language I didn't understand. Is she possessed? I wondered. What's happening?

I leaned over to my mom and asked what she was doing.

'She's speaking in Tongues," she said.

"What does that mean?" I asked her.

"She's just overcome by the Holy Spirit," she said.

"Should I knock into her? Wake her up?" I asked.

"Shhhh," my mom said.

Weird, I thought.

Another time, my mom and stepdad were out of town and they sent another parishioner to come pick me up and take me to church. Now it's just me, unsupervised, and these churchgoers. I sat as quietly as I could without drawing attention to myself and just watched the show unfold around me. People started speaking in Tongues and being knocked over by the Holy Spirit. Like, really knocked over. I sat wide-eyed while the guest pastor came out into center of the aisle and started touching people's foreheads. "Praise Jesus Almighty!" he screamed into their faces, pushing them back into the arms of someone standing behind them. Then slowly, they fell down to the ground, still speaking in Tongues.

What. The. Holy. Fuck.

He made his way through each member. I was the only one left that hadn't been touched by the Lord. If he touches my forehead, I thought, I will punch him in his Holy throat. He made eye contact with me and I suddenly felt possessed. The magical laser, I thought. Fuck! He's going to zap me with the magical laser that will change me forever.

I got up to leave and started walking out into the aisle, which clearly was mistaken for me wanting to have some hands laid on me because a big guy suddenly came from behind and pushed me forward. I stepped over the sprawled bodies, who were still mumbling incoherently. They looked like they were massacred by the Holy Ghost's evil twin.

I kept getting pushed forward, and I was simultaneously leaning back, trying to back my way out of the situation. Don't punch the minister, I told myself. The guest preacher finally stepped up to me, leaned in and shouted some "Praise Jesus Our Saviour" stuff and put his hand on my forehead. I stood there looking at him. He kept on, "Our Lord, today is the day we bow down before you..." and he pressed harder on my forehead. I stood there. He dug in hard, "We are here for YOU, our GREAT SAVIOUR!" he shouted. And he pressed so hard against my forehead I finally just gave in. Anything to end this nonsense. I raised my arms up and dramatically fell back, not even knowing if anyone was behind me. The big guy caught me and slid me down to the floor. I lay there for a few minutes, peaking out of one eye, waiting for an opportunity to crawl under the pew and out the back.

I stopped going to church after that experience, for some fairly obvious reasons. A few months went by and my mom talked me into going for Mother's Day. Begrudgingly, I went. I convinced myself to think of the scripture like a literary text, and to pretend someone was just reading a story to me. And it worked, for a little while at least. I sat in the pew, listening to my stepdad go on and on about this or that. And that's when I heard it. The one sentence that set off a fiery spark in me that has yet to be flamed out. "Wives, submit to your husbands..."

Did I just hear that right? That's his modus operandi, I thought. He serves the Lord and, in return, his wife serves him. *My mom serves him.* I was watching it happen. With church. His meals. The business. In that moment, my fierce teenage girl spirit coiled up and was positioned squarely to take on the irreverent minister. From that point on, *he* met resistance at every corner.

We were sitting at the table for dinner later that day and he started, "Lord, bless this food we are about to eat..."

And I thought, "Lord I pray this guy finds the bottle again so we can all get back to normal."

Part II
The Pursuit of Education

10
The Pursuit of Education

Despite all the new changes with my mom's re-marriage, there was one thing that remained the same. School was off the radar. To be clear, there wasn't a lack of focus on education because they saw no value in it. Or because they didn't have any respect for the educational process as a whole. Or because they couldn't be bothered with the effort it took to monitor my progress with it. Though, to a great extent, all of those were true. But more to the point, my stepfather preferred to be surrounded by people who looked up to him without questioning his ideas or philosophy. Much like the God he worshiped, he, himself, wanted to be Omnipotent.

He had strong views about school and education, often saying, "Those who do, do; and those who can't, teach." He had zero respect for teachers and dismissed any notion of me wanting to be successful in school. Good days were met with indifference. Bad days were greeted with confirmation as to why school was a waste of time. He was cynical and exuded a biting sarcasm that left you feeling some kind of way. But through his ministry, he had followers, and his ego flourished.

Parishioners showed up to the house regularly, bringing all sorts of goodies. Baked goods, home-cooked meals, and the wildly sought-after government cheese. He seemed to thrive on the impoverished, accepting their modest worldly gifts in return for his spiritual guidance. Honestly, I deeply admired the parishioners. They were authentic. Their faith was palpable. Imperfect and vulnerable, they were desperately seeking some greater good. And relief from suffering. It was relatable. I wanted it to be true for them. And it saddened me to know it was a dead end, because he wasn't taking anyone to the pearly gates.

*

Simultaneously, my dad was also knee-deep in his own situation. He re-married a woman with some interesting personality traits and unique ways of expressing her dissatisfaction. Like the time she left us on a river in Tennessee. Everything was going fine enough on our little camping trip, until she took the van and left us. My dad and I came back from a walk, and just about everything was gone. Except for her son. She took the van, supplies, her other kid, and just bolted.

Most people think that sounds terrible, that she took all of the supplies and abandoned us about a thousand miles from home. But I was relieved. Good riddance, I thought.

We spent the better part of eight hours trying to make sense of it all and piecing together some sort of plan to get back home. But she eventually returned later that night as if nothing happened, and we were all encouraged to go on with business as usual. As if we hadn't just been completely and unexpectedly abandoned earlier in the day.

Her jealousy was legendary, and it hung on a flagpole for everyone to see. It was the core of her unpredictable nature and the bane of our existence. Any amount of individual time my father spent with me was often countered with a blatant show of disapproval. Red paint dumped all over his car. Clothes thrown out of a second story window. A coffee mug thrown at his head.

Despite her antics, he continued to make an effort to see me when most guys would have abandoned ship. Chartered the much easier course. Walked away from a former life to make peace with the new. But he didn't. He pushed on when most would have quit.

I say all of that to say, both of my parents had bigger fish to fry. Burners to monitor. Fires to put out. And my education wasn't any part of that.

*

To be honest, I don't come from a long line of scholars. Our lineage is seemingly void of royal blood, war heroes, professional athletes, or anything requiring above average skill, bravery, or aptitude. I do, however, come from a long line of drinkers. Some of whom possess an extraordinary tolerance rising to the level of professional excellence. One took their drinking job so seriously that they were told to leave their home state and never come back. That is a skill of epic proportions.

*

I understood, at the time, that people in my family just didn't excel in school, let alone go to college. A few never even graduated high school. They mostly just worked. Drove a truck. Worked construction. Or put time in at the factory. It's not to say my parents didn't do well in school, because they did. Both of my parents are avid readers and my dad is a natural historian. But they didn't *excel* in any way, at least as far as I can tell. And even if they did, it wasn't likely to take them anywhere because their parents didn't expect or encourage them to go to college.

My dad did take a few college classes and did well in history and math, but he felt it would take too long to finish. His thinking was why waste time in college when he could be making money running a backhoe. And my mom said recently, "I just never thought it was an option for me."

While I was stuck in the Lord's den trying to get through high school, my brother and sister were taking college classes while simultaneously working full-time. I watched them doing it entirely on their own, with no financial help or encouragement from my parents in any way. They seemed to be making a strong go at it, and I admired them for that. Having said all of that, going to college was never encouraged, let alone expected of me.

*

Lack of support and supervision with educational activities was certainly an issue. But I was also fundamentally indifferent, overly energetic, easily distracted, and increasingly more resentful. By the time I entered high school, I had already developed years of bad habits and stifled any amount of emotionality.

Each new day brought some weird twist of events that I had to manage. As a matter of survival, I created what became known as The Denial Files. That is, a series of imaginary folders that I placed deep inside my brain. It's a place where I put all the stuff I didn't want to deal with. Or know *how* to deal with. The files essentially served as placeholders, allowing me to function enough to move through each day.

The Denial Files were like little compartments that housed all sorts of things. Anger. Abandonment. Conflict. Fear. Insecurities. Sadness. Sexuality. Bizarre events. You know, the basics. Around those Bible thumping years, the Anger File, Denial's first cousin, was at full capacity. Busting at the seams, in fact.

*

Weekends were less fun with my dad because of his stressful marital situation; and, as a result of my mom marrying my uncle, the visits with our extended family sprouted a constant barrage of insults toward them.

It was maddening.

"How's that whore of a mom doing?" an extended family member asked me one day.

"The two of them should go to hell for what they did," another chimed in.

"And how about that monkey your dad married?"

There was not just a divide between us; but rather, an unavoidable chasm. I eventually stopped going to visit them on pure principle alone. I couldn't just sit around and listen to people call my mother a whore and my stepmom a monkey. A kid has to draw the line somewhere.

*

School seemed like it was just some place I was expected to go during the day until I met some requirements and was no longer expected to go. As a result, nobody encouraged me to take challenging classes and there was never any input into what I should, or should not, be taking. So, I gobbled up all the easy classes. If there were three levels, I always said, "The bottom one, please."

*

Being an underachiever is actually harder than you think. Mostly because there are layers of potential floating under the surface, trapped beneath fear and insecurities, waiting to be tapped into by the right person or circumstances. It's a fair amount of work to keep it all hidden.

Having not done very well in middle school, I didn't have much to prove. So as a freshman, every class I had started with "General." General English. General Math. General Science.

*

But my behavior was anything but general. I organically possessed a defiance so deeply rooted that even I couldn't break myself free from it.

Especially in Home Economics. In this class, we endured laborious lectures on the principles of cooking, sewing, and budgeting. All things I fundamentally hated. I was eager to cook and taste the samples, of course; and, I remember sewing a teddy bear that I kept for several years. But otherwise, I generally refused to complete any real paper and pencil tasks.

After one particularly frustrating day, the teacher assigned me a writing punishment; whereby, I had to go home and copy 300 words on why I should follow classroom rules and be respectful toward the teacher. I did not do the writing. When she asked for it the next day, I told her I wasn't doing it. So, she assigned me double the writing for that night, of which I also did not do. We did this for two more days, until I was up to copying 1,200 words. On the fifth day she assigned me a detention, of which I did not show.

For a week, I dodged her punishments and skated through class with a 'what are you going to do now' arrogance. She was exasperated with me; and, to be fair, I don't blame her.

"That's it, Diane!" she shouted finally. "Out in the hallway for a paddling!"

A paddling? I didn't even know that was a thing. It was 1987 and I assumed paddling disappeared along with smoking in the teachers' lounge.

This oughta' be good, I thought walking out of the door. She was a tiny teacher, and I remember thinking, either way, this can't possibly hurt.

I stepped out into the hallway and she stormed out after me. I watched her walk right past me to the classroom next door. She frantically knocked on the door, and Mr Manslecky, the football coach, stepped out into the hallway. I watched her go on and on about something, waving her hands all over the place. She was so spastic about the whole thing. He disappeared back into the classroom and she came back over to talk with me. She seemed to have calmed down quite a bit. She began lecturing me about this or that, and my eyes glazed over. Suddenly, I saw Mr Manslecky pop back out of his classroom holding a paddle.

Oh shit. She can't use him to do her dirty work, I thought.

Can she?

"Is there any reason why I shouldn't do this?" he asked me holding the paddle down by his side.

The paddle was long with a half dozen quarter-sized holes in it. The handle was beautifully carved with a leather string dangling from the end. I looked at it hard. Are those signatures on there? Do students actually sign his paddle after getting hit with it? Jesus, I thought.

"What?" I said back to him.

"Is there any reason why I shouldn't do this?"

What kind of stupid question is that? I wondered. Yea, you shouldn't do this because it's going to hurt like hell!

"Do you have any medical condition or something, I mean," he said.

"Oh. No. I don't think so," I answered.

"Ok, turn around, bend over, and touch your toes," he said calmly.

Out of complete disbelieve, I did what he asked.

This is not happening right now, I thought.

Whack!

"One," he said.

The pain hit my ass and shot up into my neck and shoulders. "Shake it off, kid," my dad's words echoed in my head. The one phrase I heard a million times over from him. Anytime I got hurt, no matter how many tears were rolling down my face, my dad would come over to me, take his hand and brush it up against the injured part of my body and say, "Shake it off, kid."

Whack!

"Two," he said.

"Sha-k-e it of…" I couldn't form any cohesive thoughts.

A long pause. Then, I felt the wind of his swing.

Whack!

"Three," he said finally.

I was an absolute mess. Tears were streaming down my face. The anger was boiling up, I could feel it. I wanted to grab the paddle from his over-sized football coach hands and beat the shit out of him. Then turn around and take a few good swings at my home economics teacher for putting me in this situation.

But I refused to let them win.

"Do you need to use the restroom?" she asked me in an 'I told you so' tone.

"No," I said in between tears. "I just want to sign the paddle."

11
My Bell Jar

I ultimately survived my freshman year, but I didn't earn any accolades for my academic prowess. I continued on with my general classes. Except for English. I seemed to excel in that class.

I loved reading and writing, and my English teacher, Mrs Sardinko, caught on to that. She challenged me and I couldn't help but rise to the occasion. I discovered Catcher in the Rye. Sylvia Plath. A Separate Peace. These people came alive for me. They jumped off the pages and into my psyche. I felt Holden Caulfield's isolation and angst. I shared his disdain for phonies. I was living with one after all!

And I leapt into *The Bell Jar* with an exuberant sadness I hadn't yet found the words for. But she nailed it. Because I also wanted to be where nobody I knew could ever come. And what *was* this dark thing that slept inside? she asked. The thing I have tried to silence for years, I replied.

I wrote my life story in those daily journals. My thoughts, feelings, and fears. My dreams and desires. My deepest, darkest secrets. I even unleashed a few of the Denial Files on those pages, which I found surprisingly refreshing. And my teacher responded with lengthy red-inked commentaries that I stayed up late the night before waiting for. How would she respond? Am I crazy? Surely, they will send me away to a place for crazies. A place where deep thinkers and passionate feelers go. But you don't need to force me there, I thought. I will go willingly. Anywhere but here. Just tell me where.

*

Word spread that I had a brain and other class recommendations followed. I was a decent athlete and managed to form good relationships through sports. It channeled my energy and garnered a fair amount of positive attention.

My dad became increasingly more interested in my basketball game, and he began paying me a dollar per rebound. I was barely going to school and passing my classes, but I had a pretty good side hustle going. After games, we sat at McDonalds late into the evening, re-hashing a flawed play or obvious bad call by the referee. Hammering out details and future situations.

"You're a big girl, kid, you gotta' get in there and don't let them knock you around. You hear me?" he said handing over however many singles I earned that night.

*

Expectations and pressures mounted, though, and it became difficult to manage all the stress. Attendance and grades became important and having no real discipline or coping skills to tap into; and with all the Denial Files packed to capacity, I started to drown.

*

The day I got my driver's license was both a blessing and a curse. Prior to that, I walked to and from school. I walked home from basketball practice. And I often walked out of school on a whim. It wouldn't take much for me to reach my limit. Half-way through the day I walked down the hallway toward English, the last classroom on the first floor. The building exit was about ten lockers away from the classroom door. I stood in front of the classroom, took a deep breath. Turned, and walked right out of the door. And I *liked* English class. But it was all too much.

*

Some days I walked to school, only to find myself meandering around the neighborhood until I was sure everyone had gone to work, then walk back home. Tuck myself under the covers. And sleep. Other days I would just refuse to go altogether.

The driver's license gave me wheels to cover far more territory. Instead of going home to sleep, I motored all over town. I learned where I could buy beer in the middle of the day. It was before cell phones, so I'd buy some beer, return to school, sneak back into the building to meet up with friends, and head back out.

But then, it happened. Within two years of my mom getting re-married and our surprise upgrade to middle class, they lost everything. Including the business and the new house. We suddenly returned to our old house with less money than we started with. And through it all, my stepdad believed the Lord would provide for us. The Lord would take care of the bills, and the taxes, and the moving expenses back to our old house. With the Lord, all things were possible, according to him. Including lunch money. School supplies. And basketball shoes. Though, I don't recall the Lord ever showing up in that way. Because I had no lunch money. Or school supplies. Or basketball shoes.

The move put me farther away from school where I needed rides home from practice and games. But neither of them stepped up and it was a constant battle.

"Just quit the team," he told me one day.

Bastard, I thought. I stayed on just to spite him. Then took to organizing my own rides.

*

It was a whirlwind of chaos and right about the time when things really went downhill.

I was spending so much time at McDonalds, I got a job there. I made some new friends who were much older than me, and we started hanging out. They introduced me to the bar scene. At sixteen, things were getting worse at home and I began spending as much time out of the house as possible. Hanging out with my friends. Drinking. Ditching school every chance I got.

I managed to stay on the basketball team, thankfully, as it continued to be my only healthy outlet. One of my coaches, Mr Kelly, caught on to my troubles and offered to tutor me in Algebra. He was an older guy, and had been the boys' basketball coach for years, but was now assisting with our girls' junior varsity team. I was on varsity, so I didn't experience his abrupt coaching style first-hand. But I watched him make girl after girl cry.

Mr Kelly was a grumpy guy in his late 60's. Tough as nails. He didn't sugar coat anything. He had no problem being the sergeant standing nose-to-nose with you, screaming out all the things you were doing wrong. I'm quite certain that he saw me drowning when nobody else did. Either that, or he was incredibly bored and needed a new project.

Either way, I was failing Algebra miserably and the teacher, Mrs Alicote, was a real brut. She would draft long story problems on the board, and I'd shout out random things just to annoy her.

"Johnny falls from the roof and he's traveling 35 MPH, and on his way down he…" she said writing on the board.

"Jesus," I interrupted, "Why are you so violent in your math problems? He's dead, right? I mean, that's the answer. Johnny couldn't take math any more, so he jumped off the roof," I finished.

The entire class erupted in laughter.

Just then Mr Kelly walked into the room and I about shit my pants. I immediately sat up straight and shut my mouth. She glanced in my direction and must have sensed the fear in me. He quietly walked up to her and they stepped outside into the hallway. She came back in, looked me dead in the eyes, and donned the most sadistic smile I'd ever seen on a teacher.

Well shit, I thought.

And so, it began. Early Saturday morning tutoring sessions. Mr Kelly rang the doorbell to my house every Saturday morning at 7:30 am for two hours of tutoring before my 10:00 am basketball practice. The sessions were brutal. He stayed in my face. Forced my attention to the page. And he didn't laugh at any of my jokes.

"You're not trying," he said sternly. "Try harder," he

followed-up.

I watched him meticulously write out algebraic equations that looked a lot like hieroglyphics. Over and over, we solved meaningless equations. I was beyond bored with it.

He and Mrs Alicote quickly went into cahoots with each other. He showed up to my classroom twice per week to meet with her and get a progress report of my behavior and grades. Both were dismal.

'You need more help," he said one day after practice. And he pushed Algebra in my face like a piece of wedding cake at a reception. I couldn't escape him. He showed up everywhere. I'd be roaming the halls instead of being in class and I'd suddenly turn a corner and there he was. He didn't even work at the school.

"Oh good, I'm glad I caught you," he would say talking to me about Algebra and walking me back to whatever class I was supposed to be in. "See you after school. 4 pm."

This went on for months until the end of the semester. Finally, the teacher called us each up to her desk to give us our semester grade. I was last, which she did on purpose, I'm sure of it. B. I got a B.

She smiled and said, "Nice work. See what you can do when you apply yourself?"

As I walked back to my seat, I saw Mr Kelly out of the corner of my eye, just standing at the door. I walked over to him.

"I got a B," I said smiling.

"I know." He turned and walked down the hall. "I'll see you at practice later. Don't be late!" he said from a distance.

I got a B, I thought. And walked back to my desk. I sat down and took a long, hard breath. It was the first grade I ever earned.

*

Though appreciated, my tiny success at school were short-lived and often over-shadowed by larger chaotic situations at home. My mom and stepdad went from never being home to a permanent fixture on the couch. The extent of our conversations occurred, within my twenty step walk, through the living room on my way out the front door or back into the house on my way to my basement bedroom. And those usually went poorly.

Even though we had moved out of our new house in the nice neighborhood, it was still vacant. Nobody else had moved in. It occurred to me and my friends one day that I still had the key, and we had a house to hang out in. Me and my two best friends, Deanna and Jeri, regularly ditched school and secretly went to the house to party. One time, my sister said she had found some empty beer cans laying around, which sparked my question of, "How did you know that we were there drinking in the house?"

To which she replied, "I'm also using the house so we better coordinate."

One Friday night we decided to have a sleep over in the empty house. The utilities had been shut off, so we brought flashlights, a cooler, and blankets and pillows. It was a blast. After several hours of drinking, someone had the idea to play a game of chase around the house. In complete darkness. You could run from the kitchen, down the hallway, around through the living room, and back into the kitchen. We were a cartoon come alive. Tom and Jerry times ten. If we could have pulled off a Roadrunner stick of dynamite hallway explosion, we would have.

We were full throttle running around the house and I decided to do a sneak attack. I stopped on a dime, turned full circle, and quickly accelerated to full speed trying to surprise Jeri coming around the corner, not realizing the full impact that would happen as a result.

It's still a blur, but Jeri and I collided, and the impact was so powerful that our heads smashed into each other and my glasses got crushed up against my face, causing glass to shatter everywhere, including in my eye. I was knocked backwards with a force, landing hard on the kitchen floor. I was quickly scooped up by my drunken counterparts, and carried over to my blanket and pillow, where I eventually passed out.

Having no treatment after it happened, I woke up to complete blindness. I couldn't open my eyes. They were completely glued shut. Apparently, the blood from being cut by my broken glasses had seeped into my eyes, and having gone straight to sleep, firmly crusted them shut. I had never been blinded by dried blood before, and it was scary as hell.

I went to bed a fully sighted person and woke up completely blind.

"Oh my God," I heard.

"Quick, get some water," Jeri said.

"Shit. Ok. Yea. We got this. Wow. Ok. Shit. Yea," I heard over and over.

I blindly stumbled around the room trying to look for my glasses, as if that was the problem.

"Ok. Yea. Well. Whose idea was that anyway?" Deanna asked.

Then, a cold, wet compress over my eyes.

"Just lay down," I heard.

"I can't see. I can't open my eyes. My right eye is throbbing," I said.

"Yea, we know. Wow. Ok. Yea. We got this," I kept hearing Jeri say.

After about ten minutes of the cold, wet compress, I was able to open my eyes and make my way to the bathroom mirror.

I couldn't believe what I saw. I looked like a character in a horror film. My face was a bloody mess and my right eye was incredibly swollen. I had a large cut under my right eyebrow, which must have been where the blood was coming from.

"Oh my God," I said. "I'm going to need stitches."

"No, I think you're fine," Jeri said. "We're just going to piece your glasses back together; they're not too bad actually," she finished.

"But my eye…" I said.

The worst part was that I had basketball practice at 10:00 am.

"What time is it?" I asked.

"9:30am," Deanna said.

"I can't go to practice like this. I have to go home and show my mom. My eye is killing me," I said.

Jeri spent about ten minutes trying to piece what was left of my glasses back together. She took real pride in her work too.

They loaded all of our stuff up in the car and took me to my house while I laid in the back seat holding the washcloth over my eye.

There's a saying that true friends aren't there to make your problems disappear; but rather, they are there with you when you face your problems. They could have easily dropped me off at the door, said good luck, and left. But they didn't.

They marched me right up to the front door of my house and rang the doorbell, which seemed weird to me because I lived there. Weirder, even, is that we waited for someone to come and open the door. We were like three door-to-door salesmen waiting for the door to open, preparing our pitch, plotting our story, and reassuring each other it would be fine. But there was an underlying sadness, like the two of them just broke their favorite toy and had to take ownership for the damage. Jeri held my glasses in the palm of her hand, as if offering a holy sacrament of peace.

"Oh, my Lord!" my mom screamed upon seeing my face.

Deanna escorted me in, and Jeri followed, still holding out her offering. But she didn't get very far because she tripped on threshold of the door and dropped the glasses. What little was left of them, shattered on the ceramic tile. All of her hard work, gone.

"It's fine," she said picking up tiny pieces of glass. "No problem. Anyone have glue?" she asked in a delusional voice.

The following minutes were a verbal cluster fuck.

"We were playing football last night. Er, uh, in the dark. Yea, and out of nowhere this guy came. Well, he wasn't a guy, in a scary sense, but a kid in our class. Yea. Well not my class. Your class, right? Yea, a kid in your class. Nice really. But he doesn't have any friends. Yea, anyway, he came out of nowhere and collided with Diane who was trying to make this really awesome catch. Right? Yea, she was trying to catch the ball and…"

"Football?" my mom asked.

"Uh Huh," we said collectively like deer in headlights.

Within the hour, I was at the eye doctor. Scratched cornea. Antibiotic eye drops. A giant white patch over my right eye. And new glasses on order. But no stitches, thankfully.

If you've never had to wear an eye patch, it's an experience. It's a lot like a neck tattoo. It's entirely noticeable, and there's usually a good story about how you got it and why it happened.

My coach was very suspicious of the football story. But we dug our heels in hard, and it got better the more we told it. By the time my dad heard it, I was casually trying out for the boy's football team. Anything to escape the consequences.

12
Walking the Ledge

I plowed through my junior year of high school much like a thoroughbred horse on steroids. It was filled with unlimited adrenaline, impulsive decisions, and unbridled angst. I honestly didn't think I'd make it through the end of the year. I had a plan. I was certain that it would be my last year. And I did everything possible to make that happen.

*

The day I discovered Nelson Ledges Quarry Park felt a lot like coming home. It just made sense to me. I felt hugged by the trees and kissed by the cold air. The rocks were comfortably nestled into the earth, and the trees deeply rooted in aged soil. They were firmly grounded in their identity and purpose. Stationed for life. Destined, even. They weathered their own storms, emerging deeper in character and stronger in spirit. And I envied that. Their energy was powerful. Overwhelming, really. I could feel it. They not only made me feel strong, but they embraced me, and seemingly freed me from my troubles.

*

For those who have never been, the Ledges are located in

northeast Ohio, comprised of classic quartz and sandstone rocks that were formed after years of erosion that wore away the softer rock layers. What remains are these hard-shelled rocks that jet out, forming jagged ledges. The area can be traced back to the ice age, actually, and with its location near the Ohio River and the Great Lakes, it became a vital trade route for Native Americans, and eventually, pioneers.

Legend has it that back in the 1950's, heavy machinery dug into the cliffs and surrounding area looking for valuable resources. But instead, they hit a spring that forcefully sprouted tons of water that poured over the cliffs and down into one of the large crevices. After just a few days, the thirty-acre quarry was filled with water, leaving peninsulas, rock shelves, and an island in the middle. It became an instant magnet for free-loving hippies and high school kids looking for a place to skip school and cliff dive. And drugs. The place was famous for drugs.

On any given day, we'd make our way out there to find people laying on the rocks, or sprawled out on the tiny island, sunning their stoned bodies.

The cliff diving was spectacular. When I first saw kids jumping off the cliffs into the water, I was mesmerized. I mean, completely smashed and fearless teens make running starts and flinging their bodies out over the rocks, dropping some thirty feet into the water below. Some were wonderfully graceful while others flailed and screamed like they were just shot out of a cannon, slamming hard into the water. I was surprised some of them resurfaced afterward.

It was a beautifully dangerous place. A mecca where people of all kinds and ages came together, trying to escape their harsh realities. Parents hated it, for obviously reasons;

and, prior to us finding it for the first time, they tried desperately to have it shut down. Or at least regulated better. The quarry couldn't officially be closed because it was untouchable land caught in some bureaucratic bullshit. So, they installed a gate and fenced off the ledges and quarry section. But we quickly found a back way in by cutting a hole in the fence large enough for us to slide under.

It didn't take long for us to become regulars. We met new people. Laughed. We wasted entire afternoons out there. It was great for my friends, but it meant far more to me.

One time in particular, I came to, surprised to find my drunken legs dangling over the edge like a couple of feathers on a dreamcatcher. Though attached, they floated in the air, susceptible to the slightest environmental forces. My head, a web of chaotic thoughts. Fighting each other for dominance. They are steadfast in their job, though. Those dreamcatchers. Filtering thoughts. Turning bad dreams into good. I wish I had twenty of them, I thought. To quiet the noise, soften the blows, and sort this mess out.

The water below, a 30-foot drop, was soft and inviting. But in that moment, everything was blurry. My eyes tried hard to focus on the landscape before me. The trees. Rocks. Water. The ledge I was sitting on. This has been my second home, I thought. I find solace here. Peace. It is the only time life seems to make sense. When I'm wandering alone through the woods, dipping in and out of the earth's crevices. Feeling the mossy rocks against my skin. Breathing in the cold, heavy air. Life is real here, but it seems to land softly. Not brutally, like out there. It's easier to digest here. Manageable, even.

A few weeks earlier, I was sitting on another ledge, with no water to break a fall. Just a high cliff overlooking a dark crevice. Drunk and sad. And angry for reasons I can't quite explain. What is the point of it all? I asked myself over and over. Deep in my dark thoughts, searching for answers. Crying.

It's exhausting really. Writing your thoughts on paper, but to no avail. Journals. English papers. Poetry. Notes to friends. Music lyrics, even. Pen to paper every chance I got. Though cathartic, answers didn't jump off the page. Ever. It's as if my words fell into a black hole, taking my soul with them. I was feeling fatigued from trying to find my stride. Catch my breath. From searching for some deeper meaning to the suffering around me. If my friends hurt, I hurt. I carried their burdens as much, if not more, than they did. Not by choice. It was a disease, I thought, without a cure.

It's as if others walked around with the same drum in their head, marching to the same beat. It looked so easy for them. Badump, ump. Badump, ump. Badump, ump. It was consistent. Predictable. Satisfying, even.

But I had a different drum in my head. And it was a chaotic mess. Stuck in a mystery rhythm that took me all over the place. Badddddummmmp. Bad. Umper. Badump. Umpidy dump dump. Ump.

Take a simple thing like a research paper in history. Seems pretty straightforward, really. We were asked to write a research paper on a famous historical figure. We each marched up to the teacher's desk and declared our subject. Nine out of ten students picked a military general or former president. Makes sense if you think about it.

But not me.

"Mickey Mouse," I said confidently.

The teacher looked up at me, squinting his eyes trying to

make sense out of the pupil standing before him. Probably thinking, there's one in every class.

"Why?" he asked.

"Because Mickey Mouse makes me happy," I replied. "And he's been around forever," I added.

Long sigh. "Sure," he said. "Have a go at Mickey."

And I did, by the way, have a great go at Mickey. I learned he was instrumental in putting smiles on the faces of those living through The Great Depression. That what started as a sketch of a mouse on paper ultimately became an iconic figure recognized all over the world. He stood for all things good. Fought against evil. He showed us how to make friends, be polite, and kind. How to be brave and focus on the positive things in life. He even showed us the importance of keeping our bedroom clean.

If you can imagine, for a moment, me siting on a cliff contemplating a life-or-death decision, thinking about a god damn mouse. And I thought, if a mouse can capture the hearts of millions and transform cultures, I can survive high school.

I need to push through this, I told myself finally. And suddenly, a shift occurred. Things will be different from now on. They *must* be different. I will care less. Enjoy life more. And stop bearing everyone's burdens because I have my own to bear. And just like that, I filed those negative feelings away to a separate compartment next to the Denial Files. I called it the Lock Box.

Yes, this makes sense, I told myself at the time. In the Lock Box, they will be safe from their own destruction. *I* will be safe from my own destruction. Because I can't have these kinds of thoughts popping up when I least expect them. They need to be securely contained, in a Lock Box, directly next to my Denial Files, so I know where everything is. Denial Files and Lock Box. My own dreamcatchers, I thought. Mickey would be proud.

"Hey Asshole!" I heard from a distance. Snapped out of my thoughts, I spun my head around to follow the sound. Deanna was standing on a rock island all by herself. Jeri was laying down on an adjacent rock. Surely passed out.

"Throw me a beer!" she said.

I stood up, grabbed a lukewarm can of beer, and walked over to the ledge facing the other direction.

"Ready?" I asked

She teetered back and forth, not quite able to balance effectively. Arms stretched out wide, ready to catch the can.

I wound up, like a world series pitcher, and threw a perfect strike to her head. Except, she never moved her arms and I watched it hit her squarely on the forehead. It ricocheted off her forehead and down into the crevice, bouncing off jagged rocks, until we heard the echo of its final landing.

Thud.

I looked back up at her and she was rubbing her forehead.

"Again!" she hollered.

I went back into the case and grabbed another. This time, I announced the throw ahead of time and lobbed it to her. With one hand, she snagged it out of the air.

I watched her stumble back, sit down, open the can of beer, and drink it without interruption.

*

That was a few weeks ago. Now, I'm sitting here on this ledge, looking out over the water. With just a few weeks left of my junior year. I made it. Time to release all of those feelings. Leave it all behind. Move forward. One more year to endure, I thought. The water was calling me. For sure I can jump. I've seen others do it. I know it can be done.

I stood up and backpedaled about five feet. Just then Deanna and Jeri walked out from the woods. They took one look at me and knew what was about to happen.

"Oh shit," Jeri said.

"Diane, don't do it," Deanna implored.

Fuck it. I leaned into my steps like a true athlete, with everything to gain and nothing to lose. I let out a giant guttural scream. And jumped.

13
The Announcement

A year later I walked into the kitchen and announced, "I'm going to college." A collective set of jaws dropped, followed by silence. Eyes shifted back and forth to each other. More silence.

This statement may not seem out of the ordinary to many. But the events leading up to this decision are noteworthy. First, it was May of my senior year and I hadn't done any college preparation, other than taking the required ACT, which I scored a solid 12 on. Second, I hadn't written one essay, asked for any letters of recommendation from my counselor, or even researched any schools, let alone visit a college. Finally, I was failing Geometry, a required course for my graduation. If I actually passed and managed to graduate, I was looking at a solid 2.0 GPA. On top of all of that, I had missed about 60 days of school. Certainly, on paper, I was not college material.

Also, worthy of mention, I had been kicked out of the house a few months earlier and was living in a very poor neighborhood in a completely different school district.

My sudden change of address was a complete surprise to everyone, including me. I came home from my job at McDonald's one Thursday night in early March. I hadn't even taken my grease-stained uniform off when my mom came into my bedroom, which was really an open space in the basement;

a choice, by the way, that I personally selected as a way to keep my distance from the minister.

"There will be a truck here Saturday morning," my mom explained. "We're just out of money and the bank will be taking the house, and whatever cars they may see in the driveway. So, it's just best if you and your sister leave," she said.

"Where are we going?" I asked.

"Your brother's old house," she said.

Hearing this news was the complete opposite of winning the lottery. I knew where my brother's old house was, and it was in a different school district entirely, and a good 45 — minute drive to my current high school.

My brother's old house was a dilapidated structure that sat squarely on a warped sidewalk adjacent to a very sketchy alley. It was in a dismal neighborhood. Rundown houses were smashed up against each other. Full sized pieces of furniture were stationed on front porches, permanently occupied by stoned bodies. Small children walked around begging for food or coins. Short of the zip code, it had all the characteristics of a third world village.

The best thing this house had going for it was a five-minute walk to an iconic hot dog shop, where you could pig out on cheddar and chili dogs and wash down the hand cut fries with a milkshake, all for under five dollars. This place had an old school diner feel, with individual stools that lined the zig zag set of high counters. And a few booths to sit family style. It's probably one of the few places in that area that brought people of all backgrounds together. You knew what you were getting when you went to the hot dog shop. It was an authentic experience. And I was never disappointed. For reasons I can't explain, the thought of moving within walking distances of this place softened the blow.

Initially, I thought the move meant a complete change in school districts. With only a few months left of my senior year, I was devastated. I was a terrible student, but I was at least a well-known terrible student who had a lot of leeway. I came and went as I pleased and was rarely questioned. Some days I turned in work; while others, I was just along for the ride. I couldn't possibly transfer to another school with three months left toward graduation.

"No," my mom said. "We're just not telling anyone you don't live here any more."

"I have to keep this a secret?" I asked.

"Yes, they can't know you live in another district," she said.

"I have to drive forty-five minutes to and from school every day?" I asked knowing that I barely went as it was, and it was a ten-minute drive.

What didn't happen in that conversation was the discussion that my sister and I would be responsible for a lot of our own expenses. Food. Gas. Any miscellaneous spending money or, for me, school fees. My sister was twenty-three, working full-time at a bank, and much more prepared to move out. I was just starting my senior year softball season. I had been playing some form of baseball since I was seven-years old. Summer leagues. Varsity Softball. Every year I was on a team. But now, with this move, and added expenses, I'd be farther away from practices and games, and I needed gas money to get back and forth to school. I had to get more hours at McDonalds. There was no other way.

So, I begrudgingly quit softball, which robbed me of a

fourth Varsity letter for the sport, and I signed up for more hours at the fast-food joint.

Having no accountability that a varsity sport required, such as regular attendance and passing grades, and a commitment to refrain from drugs and alcohol; combined with zero parental supervision and a heightened resentment of feeling abandoned during a critical time in my life, it didn't take long for me to quickly go off the deep end.

From February to May of my senior year, I managed to violate just about every code of conduct imaginable. Laws were even off the table. I drove recklessly, all of the time. Fast. Intoxicated. It didn't matter. My friends and I spent more time out at the Ledges. The weather was getting nicer and we had nothing to lose. The three of us hijacked beer from drive-thru's and soared through the day with reckless abandon.

*

After one intoxicating day that started in Jeri's backyard pool, then transitioned out to the Ledges, I arrived back to my new home completely bloodied with torn clothes. My sister had just gotten home from work and found me crawling up the stairs into the house. I was completely drunk and covered in scrapes and bruises from climbing rocks and jumping off ledges. My sister, convinced I was in a car accident, or worse, assaulted in some way, was seconds from calling an ambulance.

I crawled my way up three flights of stairs and found my bed. Within minutes, I began violently vomiting all over the place. It was 4:30pm on a Wednesday. I spent the night throwing up and was too hungover to go to school the next day. My sister had a long, hard talk with me later that day, which was also around the time I realized I lost my retainer. At some point, during all of the vomiting, I must have thrown up my very expensive dental retainer.

"That's $100," my sister said. "Was it worth it?"

No, of course it wasn't worth it. That was four or five shifts at McDonalds.

In school, there were a lot of questions about me quitting the team. I was a strong hitter, and a valuable team member. People started to catch on and I didn't want to get kicked out of school, so I avoided people more and more. I tried to fly under the radar, but it was tough. My behavior was too noticeable.

I was failing Geometry, a required course for graduation. Not because I didn't have the ability, but because it was the class after open lunch. Open lunch was a time when, as a senior, you have the privilege of leaving the school grounds to go get lunch out in the community. At the sound of the bell for lunch, we would race out to our cars and tear out of the parking lot.

In the mornings before school, we snuck peach schnapps into our school bags, drove through McDonalds for some Orange Juice, then drove to school. So, for lunch, we just picked right back up where we left off.

By the time I arrived to Geometry, on the days I actually went *back* to school, I had already had a few drinks. The teacher made every effort to keep me engaged by assigning me a seat right next to the overhead projector, not realizing the heat and low buzzing sound it gave off was a sure-fire way of putting me directly to sleep.

It was a chaotic three months for me, but one of my favorite memories during that time was of our assistant principal, Mr Wipplebock. He was responsible for attendance and discipline. One random morning with just about three weeks left of my senior year, I was walking out to the parking lot toward my car. It was around 10:30am and I sat through a few classes and had enough. As I was walking, something inside me said to turn around, just to see if anyone was watching. My eyes scanned the front of the building and then, through the second story window of his office, I saw him. He was standing with his hands in his pockets. Just watching me. I zoomed in even harder. I could see his short-sleeved button-down shirt and tie. He looked more like a NASA engineer from the 1960's than he did high school principal in 1990. We both stood there, frozen in that moment, daring each other to make a move. Finally, he lifted one arm out of his pocket and waved.

I looked at him hard. Unsure of how to respond. I waved back. And then kept walking toward my car.

The next morning, I was called to his office. I sat across from him, admiring his messy desk.

"I had your brother," he started.

Here we go, I thought.

"How's he doing?" he asked superficially. "It's unfortunate, you know, how his senior year ended and all," he said shuffling some papers around.

"Uh huh," I said. It was unfortunate that, as a 10-year-old, I had to walk in the house to see my dad choking him up against the living room wall. Screaming in his face.

"You're a goddamn punk!" my dad shouted.

I remember my brother's feet up off the ground, squirming to get out of my dad's grip. My mom standing behind him telling him to calm down.

He deserved it, I suppose. Since he decided to break into

the school a few days earlier and vandalize the hell out of it. He had been running around with a group of misfits for quite some time. Most of them were members of Basement Noise. I'm sure there was a thought process involved in their decision to break into the high school in the middle of the night to break things and spray paint all over the walls. But I knew those guys like extended big brothers. They had been around the house for years. Band practice. Smoking pot. The usual. So, perhaps there was no thought process at all. Just one high guy saying to the next, "Hey, let's go fuck up the school before graduation."

And they all said yes, let's do that.

They would have gotten away with it too, except my brother all but left his signature when he spray-painted "Hi," and my sister's name on the outside brick facade. Who says hello to their sister that way?

Anyway, I don't think my dad was that pissed off about the vandalism; although, that did make the nostrils flair. I believe it was my brother calling him a terrible father that led to the gravitational choke hold.

Either way, my brother escaped charges because he hadn't yet turned 18, and he got his high school diploma in the mail. No cap and gown. No ceremony. Just a piece of paper in the mail. And some fines he had to pay with his suspected drug money.

*

"What's he doing now?" Mr Wipplebock asked again. This time, more genuine.

"Going to college for engineering," I answered. "He's

128

working too. Drafting or something at a company," I answered.

"Really?" he said raising his eyebrows as if completely blown away that he turned things around. "Good for him," he said finally.

"I guess we're late bloomers," I said sarcastically.

"Yea, about that," he leaned in. "You are on thin ice here with graduation. You're failing geometry. Your attendance it awful. And teachers don't know if you're coming or going," he said.

There was a long pause. I said nothing.

"What's going on? Is there something you want to talk about? And why did you quit softball?" he asked.

Those were a lot of questions. Did he know? I think he might know, I thought. Do I just come clean about living in another school district? I suspected they figured it out because kids talk. Everyone wants to be in the know or look like they're in the know. Kids are such phonies. You invite them to a few parties and then they rat you out afterwards. He looks like he knows. I'm sure of it. There were just a few weeks left of the school year. What could they possibly do to me?

And really, does he want to hear about my mess of a life? That I'm essentially living on my own. Driving 45 minutes to and from school, which I hate. Working to pay for food and expenses. That in three weeks I have nothing. No future plans whatsoever. Is that what I'm supposed to say?

I settled on, "I quit so that I could work more. We needed the money." Yes, that should shut him up. You can't challenge that. It's a good story. Poor kid struggling to make it in school because they're exhausted from serving greasy fries at McDonalds all night, just to get by. I liked it. I looked up at him, curious of his response.

"I see," he said moving right past that to his real agenda. "Listen," he said softly. "I talked with your English teacher, and she said you are a gifted writer. A real storyteller. That you volunteer for parts in Shakespeare. You're funny and bring things to life. It sounds like there's potential there. I hope you do something with that someday," he said kindly.

"Uh, ok," I said. For once, I was at a loss for words. I had never heard that. I've never been gifted at anything. And I have potential that I should 'do something with'? Huh.

"Also," he said. "I talked with your counselor and she said you actually don't need the geometry credit for graduation because of something else you took along the way. So, you're lucky there. But you need to pass your other classes, which you are currently; and, by the way, you've had straight A's in English since 9th grade — did you know that? I mean, four consecutive years of A's."

I nodded.

"Right, well I want to see you every day for the remaining three weeks of the year. Or no graduation ceremony," he finished sternly.

"Like, full days?" I asked.

"Diane, three full weeks. Full days. Do you understand what I'm saying to you?" he asked.

I nodded again.

*

Later that week I was standing in the hallway, taking a break from my gig in the Athletic Department, which was basically just answering phones and taking messages. I had been there for the past semester because the study hall teacher had enough of me goofing off. Instead of class, they gave me a job, which I liked very much.

Mrs. Alicote, my tenth grade Algebra teacher walked by. She stopped at the water fountain to rinse out her cup.

"Hi Diane!" she said enthusiastically.

"Hi," I replied. "Are you still writing violent algebraic equations on the board?" I asked.

"Every day," she said laughing.

"Poor kids," I said jokingly.

"What are your plans for next year?" she asked smiling.

Next year? Nobody had asked me that question before.

"College," I said quickly.

"College?" she asked. "Ha! Well, you better turn things around and get focused," she quipped. "You won't make it if you keep doing what you're doing," she added. She turned and walked off.

What the…? College? Why did I say college? Where did that come from? I have no idea what I'm doing next year. What *am* I doing? Shit.

*

The truth is, I had been getting letters in the mail from various universities on and off all year. They were all recruitment letters for basketball. I had earned some awards. Made the local paper a few times. I guess some people took notice. Not prestigious universities, mind you, but certainly accredited ones. I pulled letters from the mailbox and threw them in a stack on the kitchen counter. Every now and then I would open one and read it. It sounded exciting, playing college basketball, but it seemed so far out of my reach. I knew I didn't have any study skills and couldn't see me juggling school, work and playing ball. I just couldn't see it. I didn't even know where to begin. So, I'd carefully put it back in the envelope and return it to the stack.

*

It was later that day — the interaction with my former algebra teacher fresh on my mind that I dropped the bomb about going to college. I walked into the kitchen, declared my intentions, and then walked over to the stack of envelopes. I sifted through them, pulled out the one I thought made the most sense, and filled it out. I walked downstairs to the basement and wrote the best essay of my life. I put a stamp on it and dropped it in the mailbox. And waited.

*

It wasn't a terrible conversation, I thought. It could have been worse. Mr Wipplebock could have made a much bigger deal about me leaving school without permission. He could have used my brother against me. Or the fact I wasn't even living in the school boundary. Or a myriad of other inappropriate things I had done over the past four years. And I had done some things. But he didn't do any of that. He acknowledged some personal history to make a connection, highlighted a potential that I didn't even know I had, and gave me an opportunity that I most likely didn't deserve.

*

I didn't get berated or shamed; or worse, paddled. By my senior year, they had done away with corporal punishment. It was 1990. A new decade. The cusp of technology. A time when you could still turn in a handwritten essay and it meant something. It was before automated attendance calls home and 24-hour online grade monitoring. You waited days, or even weeks before getting a grade on something. Usually by the time I got something back, I already forgot I had done the thing. But there was a freedom in that. Wiggle room. You could walk around with an F on a paper and nobody would be the wiser. You didn't have a grade in a class until it was stamped in print. On an official report card. And even that could be modified with some fingernail polish remover and an eraser.

To be clear, I was not an easy student. On the surface, I was certifiably defiant. Steadfast in my pursuit of freedom. Purposeful in my disregard for authority. Beneath that, though, I was hurting. Hypersensitive to the suffering of others and the injustices in the world. Completely unable to manage the tsunami of emotions that wreaked havoc on my heart and soul. I was desperate to get it out. Shake it off. Go a different direction. I wanted that. I *needed* that.

I remember the teachers who listened to me. Gave me the creative freedom to express my ideas and granted me the permission to make them laugh. They didn't just put up with me for the class period; but rather, they embraced all that I brought to the table. And encouraged it. Let me play a part in Shakespeare. Write a research paper on Mickey Mouse as a major historical figure. And responded to my bizarre journal entries with thoughtful words of encouragement. That it was ok. That *I* was ok.

But mostly, I remember a profound freedom and connection with the school staff whereby they seemed to say, "You're a mess, we see that. But you're OUR mess and we will be here for you every day. Whenever you're ready."

And this, I believe, got me to the finish line. Because I did, in fact, make it the full three weeks. For Mr Wipplebock, Mrs Alicote, and Mrs Sardinko. For all of the teachers who reached out. Put up with my antics. Laughed at my jokes. I also did it for me. And my family, even. Without knowing it at the time, it was one of my first steps toward becoming the first generation of normal. As such, I proudly walked across the stage to receive my high school diploma. I flipped my tassel and wondered if anyone had read my college essay yet.

14
College

On my very first day of college, I wrecked my car. It's as if the universe thought my life was too boring; that, for some reason, I hadn't had enough challenges to overcome. To be fair, I was a terrible driver. Even when focused. Which I was, very focused, at 6:00 AM on that dark, rainy morning. I could not have predicted that at some point in the early morning hours, while I was still lying in bed staring at the ceiling, wondering what college was going to be like; that a guy would stumble out of a bar, too drunk for rational thought, get in his car and try to drive home. And that, after some time behind the wheel, he would decide to pull over and take a nap. Sleep it off.

Only he didn't quite pull completely over. He left his rear end out, just enough so that my big front end of a car could smash into it. That rear end was just sitting there. Dark. Taunting me. As if to say, so you think you're going to college and getting out of here, eh?

SMASH!

I never saw the car. He sat in complete darkness. Car shut off. No hazard lights. It was early morning hours kind of dark, and rainy. A two-lane road with no streetlights. And he had no lights on in the car whatsoever. And because I never even saw the car, I never applied my brakes. A 35 MPH sudden impact that jolted him awake and me back to the reality of my station in life. Nothing is easy. Ever.

He stumbled out of the car like, well, like he had just gotten hit by a car going 35 MPH. I made my way out of the car, still in shock from the sudden impact. It was pouring down rain. But the sun was beginning to rise, giving us enough light to take stock of the situation. I stood, staring at his car. His rear end looked like it was about to find a second home in the junk yard. I looked back at mine.

At the time, I was driving a 1978 powder blue Pontiac Firebird. A surprise gift from the minister, which I suspect came with an ulterior motive. If you have wheels, you will leave the house. Nonetheless, the gift was appreciated because I did, in fact, need wheels and left the house. The thing about that car is that it is ALL front end, with a little space to sit in the cockpit. Zero room in the backseat and trunk. I scanned the car. It handled the impact like a champ. The right front fender was smashed, of course, but drivable. Good, I thought. I can still make my 08:00 class.

The guy didn't say much. He looked at the back of his car. Walked over and looked at my front end. Mumbled a few words. Got back in his car. And drove off.

What the—? Is he leaving the scene? No cops? No million-dollar lawsuit? There's a story here, I thought. He didn't want the cops called. Obviously. I crawled back into my car and let it all sink in for a minute. Took a deep breath. Started the engine. And made my way to the campus.

About fifteen minutes before my first class, I found a payphone and gave my dad a call to tell him about the accident. It was before cell phones when a quarter could make a difference between life or death. Upon hearing the news that I smashed into a parked car on the side of the road, he yelled so loud that I had to hold the phone away from my partially deaf ear. I tried to explain the situation, but his response was way over the top. I hung up on him. One quarter, wasted. I grabbed my brand-new backpack filled with all sorts of notebooks and highlighters, and hauled it across campus to begin a new journey.

Youngstown State University was, at the time, predominately a commuter school. The majority of students drove to and from campus daily. Nobody I knew lived in a dorm on campus. It was a good college to work your way through. As in, you had to work to pay bills and go to school, or you had to work out some issues, or you just had too many issues to go to any other respectable university. I checked all of those boxes.

Students today meticulously line up their college choices as either a dream, target, or safety school. I hear students use these words every day. They are defined by them. And I secretly feel sad about it because you can hear the inflection in their voice ebb and flow with each potential option.

A dream school is the long shot. A pie in the sky idea. It's the, *my family will be so proud of me*, school. And they announce the name with such enthusiasm that I can almost see them enrolled, taking classes there, and loving it. Graduating. And moving on to do great things in life. Such bright eyes and love for life.

A target school is the socially accepted school. Usually a more subdued tone, with a hint of insecurity tagging along. This is the school most in line with their skill set and educational record. It's the sweet spot, really. It's the *I'll be ok in life* school.

The safety school is always last, and said in a *this is what people keep telling me to do but if this happens my world will be over* tone. There's an underlying sense of embarrassment and denial attached. Disappointment, even. As if they are too proud to need a safety net.

But having this selection process makes sense really. It's smart. Respectable, even. It shows you have options and are carefully weighing each and every one of them based on a variety of factors and feedback you get from those around you.

Having said all of that, Youngstown State University, for me, was my desperate school. In that, I was feeling hopelessly desperate because, quite frankly, no other accredited school would take me in June, a month after I graduated high school, with a transcript as dismal as mine. It is possible; however, that they received one letter of recommendation from an almost-retired teacher who, indiscriminately wrote, please accept this wayward youth into your college so they become a decent human being and certified tax-paying citizen. Lord help us all.

Before I even stepped foot onto the campus, I had already negotiated a handful of obstacles in a short amount of time. First, I had to secure a job that didn't leave me smelling like greasy French fries every night. I managed to get a job working in the sporting goods department at a major retail store. It was a small pay increase, with incentives for selling bogus extended warranties. And, the store was conveniently located halfway between school and my house. It was an upgrade, for sure.

Second, I had to break away from all things that could interfere with me moving forward. Bad habits. Poor choices. Toxic relationships. Having lived on my own for several months, I had acquired a good amount of all of those. Within a few short weeks, I ended a high school relationship, sent my best friend off to boot camp, and cut ties with my mom and the minister.

All were necessary so that I could focus and devote the time and energy to my schoolwork. To be clear, though, the high school relationship was doomed from the start. But his lack of direction sealed the deal. I was just starting to figure things out, and couldn't possibly do it for the both of us.

And boot camp happened, not because of Deanna's desire to serve her country; but rather, as a result of me kicking her out of the porch she had been sleeping in for the past few months. This left her homeless, for the second time in just two months. Because shortly after high school, her mom kicked her out of the house and abruptly changed the locks. And not having anywhere else to go, I offered her our front porch. It was enclosed, of course. I'm not entirely cruel. But it was tiny, and sat uneven on its shaky foundation, just off the sidewalk of a busy alley. The space was so tight that, with each passing car, you held your breath they didn't drive right up into the porch. If you were quiet enough, you could hear conversations *in* the car as it crept by. And for sure, you heard every argument erupting in the alley and adjacent houses.

My difficult decision to kick her out happened because I woke up several mornings in a row to find a handful of strangers sprinkled around the living room, entirely passed out. The room wreaked of pot and stale beer. My sister was not having it, and Deanna would have none of someone telling her what she could and could not do.

"You can't stay here any more," I said. "You need a plan."

Eight hours later she came home with enlistment papers for the Navy.

Well shit.

"I just meant you couldn't stay here because I'm going to school in the fall. I didn't mean you had to go off to war, you asshole," I said slurring my words and crying to her one night.

"Just help me pass my piss test," she laughed.

As far as my mom went, communication with her and the minister rapidly declined after I was abruptly kicked out of the house four months earlier. There were no visits or phone calls to check on me. And I was fine with that. Less emotional drama to manage, I thought.

And finally, I had to figure out how to pay for college. With my dad newly divorced, he inserted himself back into my life like a new wart on my knuckle. You've had it before. You know what it's about. And though mostly harmless, it's inconvenient as hell.

After a lot of behind closed-door conversations, some kind of deal was struck. It's as if my dad emerged from the rubble with a renewed enthusiasm for the next leg of an ultramarathon through the mountains. He was ambitious. Sure-footed. And stern. Daunting, even.

"I'll cover your tuition, kid. But you can't get anything less than a B. Do you hear me? A's and B's," he said.

My jaw dropped.

"And I'm not paying for all those expensive books, or your gas to get there, or any of your other stuff," he grunted. "You're going to have to figure that out for yourself," he finished.

And just liked that, he plucked us out of the dilapidated house in the back alley and moved us to one of his rentals, just down the street from where he was living. "So I can keep an eye on you," he claimed.

It was a solid house that made up the bottom, right corner

of a triangle of rentals he owned at the time. Jammed in tight, the three of us shared one driveway. It felt nice, though, to lay down in a structure without feeling like you might slide into a black hole with one gust of wind. Or get murdered walking out to your car. It had a lot of charm and character, our new place. My sister took to decorating it like it was her own. And I settled into a small, upstairs bedroom overlooking the house my dad lived in when I was a kid. Forest green in color, it also backed up to an alley. I spent a lot of nights in that house, wondering if the alley ghosts would come get me while I slept.

Sometimes the greatest motivation in life is someone who doubts you. Particularly if you're competitive and have nothing to lose. So, when my dad offered to help pay for my college tuition, on the condition I didn't get anything lower than a B, I jumped on it. Of course he offered that because he never in a million years expected that I *could* get anything better than a C. He was confident my run at college would be short-lived. To be fair, that's all he knew of me. That I was a C and D student, predominately. Either way, I accepted his challenge and prepared for the ultramarathon that would take me out of there.

As I moved swiftly across campus on that first morning, scanning the campus map in search of my first class, I glanced at my watch. 7:55. Shit. I shouldn't have stopped to call my dad. Now I'm going to be late. First the accident, then the terrible phone call, and now my poor sense of direction. Suddenly, I saw my building from a distance and kicked it into high gear. I don't think I've ever moved so fast to get to a class in my whole life. I did not want to be late. This was my chance, I thought. From now on, it will be different.

7:58. I rushed into the building and immediately opted for

the stairs. Two at a time. 7:59. I turned the corner and found my classroom. Students were filing in. I impatiently waited my turn.

8:00. I walked into the room and grabbed the first open seat. Sat down. Took a deep breath. Pulled out my notebook. And wrote English 550 on the cover.

15
Living with a Mob Boss

Starting college was stressful, but my sister helped me pick college classes she thought I might be good at. She encouraged me to stay in the English and Psychology family as much as I could, then knock out some electives, and stay away from math, science and history as long as possible. It was good advice.

And my brother gave me a second-hand computer, which I didn't even know I needed. He carried it up to my bedroom. Set it up. Connected it to a printer. And taught me how to use it.

I eventually had to take Geometry, the class I failed my senior year, and managed to get an A. In fact, much to everyone's surprise, I earned all A's and B's my entire first year of college.

School was going very well but my sister decided to get married and take over the house we shared. We had lived together, just the two of us, for almost two years. She always had my back, supported me going to school, and lectured me when I got out of hand. That doesn't include her pseudo-parenting me as a kid. She had been trying, in fact, to just keep me alive for most of my life. Her job was done.

And just like that, I was displaced for a third time in the span of two and a half years. It was decided that I would move into an upstairs apartment above my father. Except for my first two years of existence, I had never lived full-time with the guy. He came in and out of my life like a firestorm. But there were always beaks in between visits, providing respite from his intensity and an opportunity to decompress. As such, I had a great deal of trepidation about the move. At the time he showed me the space, it was completely unfinished. It was a real shambles. "Don't worry, kid, I'm going to fix this up real nice for you," he said.

And he did. So nice, that most of my friends were jealous of the place.

But living with my father was a lot like being on a reality television show; whereby producers who were trying to make a name for themselves, crafted outrageous scripts and spontaneous obstacles, just to see my reaction.

For example, shortly after I moved in, he went about bolting safety things to the floors and door frames. Out of an abundance of caution, he bolted a fire escape ladder to my second story kitchen floor, put a deadbolt on the door itself, and then made his way to my front door where he bolted a twenty-pound chain on to the door frame.

The apartment was situated on a corner lot, with the back of the house smashed up against the neighboring house. There was a narrow driveway and small garage separating the two. I had a back door off the second story kitchen. It was just a door that, when you opened it, went nowhere. There were no stairs leading to the ground. So, if you opened the door and stepped out, you'd fall about 15 feet to the ground.

When he put a deadbolt on the door, I was perplexed. "Dad, nobody can get in here. There aren't any stairs and spider man, isn't really a thing," I said.

"You can't be too careful around here," he replied as he flipped the deadbolt knob back and forth on a door that went nowhere.

I appreciated his concern for my safety, but then he insisted that I practice using the chain and fire escape regularly.

On any random day he'd walk by my apartment door and check to see if the chain was connected. If I didn't have the chain on, and the door opened, he would rush into my apartment and shout, "Let's give it a go, kid. There's a fire, what are you going to do?" he asked rushing me through the apartment toward the fire escape.

"Are you for real right now?" I asked. "I'm 19 years old dad. This seems silly," I said instantly realizing that was a mistake.

"Oh, is it silly to burn to death in a fire? Huh?" he asked sarcastically.

So off I went.

He watched me unbolt the Door to Nowhere, fumble with the roped ladder, hesitantly slide my body out onto the thing, and slowly climb down to the ground.

"You took so long because you were running your damn mouth!" he shouted from up above.

Then came the used appliances. In an effort to outfit my new apartment, he brought a variety of used goods into the house.

"Look what my dumpster-diving buddy salvaged for us," he said proudly holding a small microwave. "Just give it a good clean, kid. It'll work just fine."

He set it on the counter and left.

I took to fumbling around with it a bit. Plugged it in. And

just as I was about to grab a rag, a cockroach popped out of the back.

"Shit!" I screamed.

Then another one popped out. And before I could blink, there were a half dozen cockroaches zipping around my kitchen.

"Dad!" I screamed. "Jesus-fucking-Christ!"

*

A few weeks later, he showed up with a used refrigerator.

"I know your last fridge shit the bed, kid," he said. "This one's a bit used, so you'll have to just get in there and scrub it real good," he said knowing how much I hated cleaning.

Still reeling from the cockroach incident, I implored him to give it a thorough inspection.

I opened the door and it was like a dismembered body was stored in there for safe keeping. The smell about knocked me over.

"Oh, hell no," I said shutting the door.

I glanced over at the door to nowhere. Maybe I'll just jump and call it a day. Anything so I don't have to clean this disgusting refrigerator.

"Oh, you're too good for something used, eh?" he screamed in my face.

"Dad, this is not just used, it's foul. Disgusting. I don't want it," I shouted back at him.

"Well, too bad," he said throwing me a rag.

"Take it back!" I screamed throwing the rag back at him.

And so it went on and on. We had probably one of our largest arguments of our lives that day, all over a refrigerator.

But ultimately, the refrigerator stayed. As did I, at least for a little while longer.

Living with my father also meant I couldn't use any heat to stay warm during the frigid northeastern Ohio winter months. He kept a close eye on the furnace usage, to the point I kept just about every article of clothing I owned on. All of the time. It was just easier that way. One time I had some friends over and turned the heat up so they could comfortably take off their winter coats. It was about sixteen degrees outside, and the inside temperature hovered around a balmy 60 degrees Fahrenheit. A few hours into the gathering, the entire floor began to vibrate. A picture fell off the wall. "Turn the music down!" Someone shouted. And then we heard it.

Thump! Thump! Thump!

The thumping vibrated up into our feet. I walked downstairs to investigate. I found my dad, sitting in his half-broken recliner, holding a beer in one hand, and one of the largest lead pipes I'd ever seen in the other.

"What are you doing?" I asked.

"Tell your friends to put their coats on and turn that thermostat down," he replied. And then he jammed the lead pipe into the ceiling three times.

Thump! Thump! Thump!

"Jesus Christ, you're bat-shit crazy! It's sixteen degrees outside!" I shouted walking back upstairs.

The thumping continued throughout my stay with him. If he heard the furnace kick on any more frequently then he thought it should, he grabbed the pipe and jammed it hard into the ceiling. That's why I was surprised one hot July night, when the pipe thumping occurred. I was deep into a project for school, frantically trying to meet a deadline. There was no air conditioning in the apartment so it was unbearably hot. It wasn't uncommon for temps in the upstairs apartment to escalate into the 90s on a muggy, July night. So obviously, I wasn't doing anything related to the furnace. I had just been sitting on the floor with an ice pack on my neck trying to stay cool when my ass suddenly vibrated. I immediately went downstairs to see what was wrong.

I found him sitting in his makeshift office, surrounded by tall stacks of unopened mail.

"You want a beer?" he asked.

"Really?" I asked.

"C'mon, you're just sitting around up there not doing anything. Sit down and have a beer with your 'ole man'," he pleaded.

"Dad, I'm working on a project that's due tomorrow," I replied.

"I'm going to be gone one day and you'll wish you spent more time with me," he said desperately.

Will I? I thought. But I stayed and had a beer with him. Not necessarily because I wanted to; but mostly, because it was the quickest way for me to get back to my project.

Probably the most annoying thing about living above my father in that upstairs apartment, other than the unprecedented levels of extreme temperature variations — 60 degrees in the winter to one hundred in the summer — was the unpredictability of odd jobs I was often called upon to assist with. It was always one precarious situation after another. And it didn't matter what I was doing at the time. I would have my books and class notes spread out all over the floor, trying to study or complete some assignment, and, "Hey kid! Come down here for a minute!"

Four hours later, I'd be free to return to my studies.

On one of those missions, I was coerced into accompanying him over to one of his properties late one night after he evicted the tenants. "I just gotta' see what they left me, kid," he said pulling into the driveway. We opened the door and, using only the moonlight at first to find our way in, I felt like the floor was moving. The foul smell immediately hit my nostrils and I closed my eyes in disgust. I stood still in the dark, plugging my nose, and felt the floor moving beneath me.

As soon as my dad turned the lights on, we saw the entire floor, covered in black cockroaches, begin to move. They scattered so fast it made me dizzy. Every bit of the floor and counters were covered in cockroaches.

"Jesus Fucking Christ!" I screamed.

Within seconds they were all gone. Disappeared completely. Trekking through the walls and floorboards, looking for places to hide.

Bastards, I thought.

"Yea, kid," my father said laughing, "you won't forget this one."

*

Some of the chores I brought on myself. Like the one time my friends wanted to go to Florida for spring break. I needed about $150, of which I did not have. So, I offered to do some work around his properties to earn the cash.

"Oh, I got work for you," he said.

First, he had me scrape and paint the detached garage. After the third day he said, "What the hell is taking you so long?"

"Dad, I'm carrying 16 hours of coursework. I have a lot of stuff going on right now," I said.

"Oh, so you just do this whenever you feel like it, huh?" he asked sarcastically.

Then came the attic job; whereby, he sent me without any protective gear whatsoever, to rip out old asbestos-filled insulation. That also took about three days. The job left me covered in black soot and coughing up a lung.

Finally, to round out my spring break money-seeking adventure, he took me up a three-storey ladder onto his roof and instructed me to pull off all of the shingles in preparation for new ones that he was going to lay the following week. He handed me a crowbar and then left to do another job. About an hour into it I got hungry, so I went downstairs to make myself a sandwich. I got a few bites in when he stormed up the stairs into my apartment.

Dammit, I thought. The chain.

He busted into my apartment hollering, "A lunch break already?"

"I just want a god damn sandwich!" I yelled back.

He made me leave my half-eaten sandwich on the counter and go back up to the roof. For the next four hours, I rambled on and on about the sandwich while pulling shingles off the roof. "I wish I had a sandwich… la la la…" I'd sing. Or I just made-up stories. "Once upon a time a girl made a sandwich and the Big Bad Wolf came in and said, I'll huff and puff and blow that sandwich right out the window!" I said.

"Jesus Christ shut up about the sandwich," he said waving his crowbar at me.

"You know," I replied, "Adam and Eve didn't get into trouble over an apple. It was really a ham sandwich. Can you believe that?" I asked him.

Finally, when my three jobs were done, which he claimed were not completed to a level of professional quality, he took me down to his basement to sort out the payment. I sat in a metal chair, admiring the enormous amount of clothes he had strung about the space. They were clearly hung over the line soaking wet, and with the freezing temperatures still in the air, they froze in that position. Everything was rock hard. I walked over and lifted a frozen towel off the line, and it remained folded exactly as it was.

I just looked at him in disbelief.

"Real men use towels that cut their face," he said sternly.

*

Cobwebs hung from every part of the ceiling. A toilet set out in the open. A roll of toilet paper hung on a homemade wooden handle that jetted out from a two by four bolted to the wall. Duck taped to the board was a string, with a pencil attached.

What in the world is he writing while sitting on the toilet? I wondered.

"I like what you're doing with the place," I said sitting back down on the cold, metal chair. I could see my breath.

He glared at me.

"Ok," he went on. "Three jobs, of which took way longer than they should have. Sorry kid, I'm just telling it like it is," he said matter of factly.

"Uh huh," I replied.

"You're going to really appreciate that college degree once you get it. And you need it because you're not cut out to do manual labor," he said looking at me with flared nostrils.

"What's the total?" I asked.

"Yea, ok," he said writing out numbers with a pencil he clearly sharpened with a pocketknife. "About twenty hours, at minimum wage … that's $4.25… so that's $85," he said.

"What? That's it?" I asked. "That's not even enough for me to go," I implored.

"Minus," he started, "how many breaks did you take? I mean, I could deduct all of those… Plus, I have to re-do that section of the garage you fucked up," he went on.

"Fine, I'll take the $85," I said begrudgingly.

He reached into his first wallet and flipped through some small bills, closed it, and returned it to his back pocket. Then he reached for the thick wallet chained to his belt loop. He opened it and a fat wad of cash spilled out. I never saw so much cash in one place. I watched him thumb through several hundred-dollar bills, skipped right over them, and then meticulously laid out the $85, one small bill at a time.

*

From the day I moved in with my father, the neighbor behind us kept his incessantly barking dog on a short chain in the back of his house. He didn't take very good care of it and it was painful to watch. The guy was sketchy and had a stream of teenage kids coming and going from the house all hours of the night. We suspected there was a fair amount of drug dealing happening and my father advised me to stay the hell away from the guy. But the dog never stopped barking.

One day I came home from class and the dog was gone. It was the quietest my little apartment had ever been. I stood in my kitchen, staring out the door to nowhere, looking into the neighbor's backyard. The chain lay there, with no dog attached. He was gone. Suddenly, there was banging on my front door. Thankfully, after months of practicing drills with my father, it became routine for me to put the 20 lb. safety chain across my door. I peered out the window at the top of my stairwell and saw the crazy neighbor on my tiny stoop.

Bang! Bang! Bang!

Just then my dad popped out of his door, which was adjacent to mine, and I saw them exchanging words. The neighbor looked pissed.

My dad stood firmly, shrugged a bit, looked around to the other houses, pointed at a few things off in the distance, and walked the neighbor back to his property. If it's one thing about my dad, he doesn't ever back down. In fact, he doubles down and then makes you feel silly for bringing the thing up in the first place. I could tell the neighbor wasn't quite sure what just happened. And I empathized with him for a moment because I knew exactly how he felt.

Later that night, my dad showed up to my apartment half drunk. He walked into my kitchen, pulled a cold beer out of the refrigerator, and stared out the door to nowhere.

"Quiet, huh?" he asked. He took a few more sips of his beer. "It's nice," he said staring at the empty chain that used to have a dog attached.

He came back into the living room and sat down. We sat in the quiet for a moment.

"Dad," I started. "Um, did you, you know, do something to that dog?" I asked.

"Hell no," he replied instantly. "That guy is crazy. You just stay the hell away from him, you hear me?" he said sternly.

There was a long pause.

"It's nice and quiet though, isn't it?" he asked again.

Shit. He did do something to that dog, but he doesn't want to tell me so the guy can't beat it out of me when he snags me from my car late at night, holding me at knifepoint, asking where his terribly neglected dog went. It was clear my dad was protecting me from whatever occurred between him and that dog. I was sure of it.

I kept sneaking glances at him, in the shadows of my moonlit apartment. Slowly sipping on a beer like a Mob boss in the corner of an Italian restaurant. Slurping spaghetti and drinking cheap red wine. Giant gold ring on his pinky. Sitting in the satisfaction, of strapping some concrete blocks, to a suspected police informant's, feet. Pushing him off a dock. Wiping his hands. Annoyed that he was late for dinner. A deed well done. A situation resolved. I could see it in his eyes. I felt it. It had nothing to do with what my father said in that moment, as much as what he didn't say. The unspoken truth he wanted me to know but didn't want me to hear.

*

Years later, I asked my father about the missing dog. He finally admitted that he did, in fact, take the dog for a long drive out to the country and let him run free. "Trust me, kid, that dog was so happy to be let loose," he said. "I don't regret it one bit. But I know the guy knew it was me. That's why I told you to stay away from him. I knew he would try to get back at me. That's why I never complained about the damn barking," he went on. "I didn't want to complain, then have the dog mysteriously disappear, you know? I just played it real cool, then late one night, I knew he wasn't home. I just walked into his backyard with some bolt cutters and a few pieces of cheese. That dog jumped into my car so fast," he said.

My dad *is* a Mob boss, I thought.

PART III
All Grown UP

16
Popsicle Sticks and Velcro

"Are you our new teacher?" the bright-eyed thirteen-year-old asked. "Because we ran those other punk-ass bitches outta here in no time," he said before I could answer.

It was a fair question. And one that I didn't, yet, have the answer to.

*

At 9:00 AM the day before, I walked into a historic building on the east side of Cleveland, Ohio for a job interview that changed my life and defined the trajectory of my career. Opening that door kick started what would become a 25-year journey in public education. I walked through those doors and was immediately blown away by its architecture. I couldn't help but wonder what untold stories were held captive inside the walls; or rather, what stories I would become a part of and share with others. I felt some kind of way about it and I couldn't have been more intrigued.

It was February of 1996, I was newly married and just applied to my first teaching job at a school that only accepted students who had been kicked out of every other school. I was ready to change the world and nothing was going to stop me. I was an idealistic, peace-loving, anti-war, everyone is free to be, white girl hippie.

Since I attended college in Youngstown, Ohio, I did the majority of my educational field work in the surrounding schools. Youngstown, once referred to as Murder Town USA, is a true midwestern city in what is known as the Rust Belt, an area hit hard by deindustrialization in the late 1970's. The closing of steel mills led to economic decline, population loss, and overall urban decay. And a notoriously high murder rate per capita. It was also known for the Mafia. Though the mob all but disappeared in the mid-1980's, there were still pop — up car explosions and attempted assassinations every once in a while.

In 1996, the year I graduated college, there was an attempted assassination on an outspoken anti-mafia politician, named Paul Gains. Shortly before he was to take office as county prosecutor, intruders broke into his home and shot him. He miraculously survived, and the investigation led to a top gangster in town. Something out of a movie, really.

Also, at the time I was attending Youngstown State, and prior to getting married, I was living with my own mob boss.

I say all of this to say, I was not naive. I had been exposed to a wide range of people and lifestyles. I had experienced things. Seen things. Life had not been easy. I commuted to college in a car that had a driver's side door so rusted out, it was virtually impossible to lock yourself out of because there was a hole large enough to stick your entire hand right through the thing. I worked part-time to pay bills. I walked to Christie's, a small corner store with a plexiglass shield around the cash register, to buy potato chips and dip for dinner. I had neighbors who never left the comfort of the couch on their front porch.

So, when I arrived at my interview on the east side of Cleveland, I felt like there wasn't much that I couldn't handle. An older gentleman greeted me, "I'm Mr James," he said holding out his hand.

"Diane Ross," I said expecting the usual reaction. Every time I said my full name out loud, there was almost always a comment related to Diana Ross and the Supremes. I waited. Nothing. I like this guy, I thought. He doesn't like low hanging fruit.

He invited me to follow him down a large, dim hallway, to a small room with two school desks. That was the extent of the room — two school desks. It was just the two of us. Everything seemed to echo, which alarmed me. It all seemed so empty and cold. I wasn't sure if this was going to be an interview or interrogation.

I was wearing an inexpensive suit and carried a portfolio of all the tedious work samples my education program said I needed to have. I followed him into the dreary room and wondered if it was enough.

Mr. James was a pale guy. His whiteness blended into his light grey suit. It was hard to say where one stopped and the other started. But he had an edge to him that I couldn't quite understand. He wasn't intimidating in any way, but he knew things that I hadn't yet learned. And he took pride in that fact.

It was just the two of us. He led with all of the expected interview questions. Why are you here? What are your goals? What kind of work experience have you had?

They were simple questions. Because I need a job. To change the world. I've worked before.

How did you hear about us? he asked.

The Plain Dealer, I replied.

I remember it vividly. Driving through my run-down town late one night, I thought, we need to get out of here. I had finished my coursework a month earlier and was working as a substitute teacher at various schools. Because I finished my program in December, I didn't have many options since it was the middle of a school year. Substitute teaching was the worst for me because they call you at 5:30 in the morning and ask you if you want to work. Who wants to work at 5:30 in the morning? Every day is different, and you don't have time to build any relationships so it's like you just keep starting each day over and over. For that reason, I declined more jobs than I accepted. I did this for about a month, then bought a newspaper and scoured the Classifieds. Finally. I highlighted the following:

Seeking aspiring teacher who wants to make positive changes in young people within a diverse setting. Must be flexible and open to challenges. We will train you. Position is available immediately. Competitive Salary Package.

Perfect, I thought.

As I sat in my very first professional interview, I tried really hard to stay focused. My mind kept wandering all over the place. How old is this guy? Where is everyone else? Am I his only interview today?

I didn't think it was going particularly well, but he must have seen something in me because he leaned into his questions like someone on a first date. Skeptical, yet gauging every utterance and move. Are you *the one*? Heightening his performance to capture my attention, then easing back into the, 'We're just here to get to know each other routine.' It was confusing for me. One minute it was intense, and the very next casual.

I answered his questions as he liberally applied Chapstick to his seemingly moist lips. The Chapstick. It was a thing. And it was weird to me.

All of a sudden, he leaned in close and said, "What is about to happen is part of the interview." Then he sat back in his chair.

Oh shit, I thought. He's going to murder me.

Before I knew what happened, he leaned back in just about an inch from my face and screamed, "You mother fucking, cock-sucking, sonnofabitch, whore!"

The spit flew out of his mouth like a broken sprinkler, making it impossible to dodge.

"And fuck you!" he screamed while pushing back away from me, standing up, and full on drop-kicking his chair across the room.

Ok, that had to hurt, I thought.

To be honest, I took the cursing. And spit. I didn't even wipe it away because I was so locked into whatever he was selling. I wasn't aware of a protocol for this situation. The university did not prepare me for this moment. Do I swear back? Spit back? If I do nothing, do I bomb the interview? He must expect me to *do* something. It must be a test for sure. Or has he completely lost his mind? What if he *is* psycho and it's not about the interview at all and how I respond is the difference between life or death?

*

"Um," I hesitated, "I've never been called a whore before. So that's a first," I said.

"I'm just curious, will there be a follow up interview to this?" I asked. "Or, you know, is this it?"

*

"These are the kind of explosive behaviors you'll encounter in this position," he said calmly as he sat back down in the chair he retrieved from across the room. "And yes, there's a follow-up interview at the school with the principal, Mr Johnson, should you be interested," he said liberally applying chap stick to his lips.

"Sure," I said. "I'm interested." How can I not be interested? I've never been so curious. About this guy. The school. The kids with these apparent explosive behaviors.

He handed me the school's address, "It's in Shaker Heights," he said. Then he handed me his business card. You call me after the visit and let me know if you are still interested in the position. We like to train our staff so don't worry if you don't feel completely up to speed right away. This interview is really about gauging a person's temperament," he revealed. "You passed."

I passed the interview and he never once looked at my portfolio.

The following morning, I drove down Shaker Boulevard and was mesmerized. Large Tudor homes sat on beautifully manicured lawns. The brick walkways and winding driveways added flair to their elegant facade. They were the largest homes I had ever seen. *Who* lives in these houses, I wondered.

I got deeper into the neighborhood and saw the front of the school from a distance. It was a large, brick school, blending well into its surrounding community. The second story large windows towered over the smaller arched first floor windows. An ornate stone door frame marked the front entrance. I pulled around to the back of the school and parked. I left my portfolio in the back seat and walked toward the door.

The principal greeted me at the door. "Mr Johnson," he said with a smirk.

"The other teachers left rather abruptly," he told me as we walked through the hallway to the main office.

He was a big, stocky guy, and if you took a picture of him and held it up next to the Reverend Dr Martin Luther King Jr, you'd have a hard time distinguishing Reverend from Principal.

"Get the fuck out of my face!" I heard off in the distance. Followed by a loud door slam. We turned a corner and two large men ran past me with radios.

I turned to watch them move swiftly down the hallway.

A few seconds later, I saw a young man outside a classroom kicking the door to get back in. Another student came from around the corner at full speed. "Leave me the fuck alone!" he was screaming to everyone. He didn't seem bothered by the fact he was only wearing one shoe.

A very tall man was on his tail, holding the other shoe.

"It's a busy day here," Mr Johnson said matter of factly.

"Uh huh," I responded spinning my head around.

Just as we started to approach the main office, I looked to my left and saw this beautiful foyer with stained glass windows on the doors. Inside, two adolescent male students stood talking to an adult male. One of them saw me and immediately lunged at the door, "Oh hell yea!" he shouted. The staff member quickly grabbed his arm to keep him from opening the door.

"Bitch, what's your name?" the other one joined in as he shoved his face up against the glass.

What… the… fuck, I thought, quickly returning focus back to the safety of the main office.

We continued on into his office and sat down. "Mr James thought you would be a good fit for the position. You're from Youngstown, is that right?"

"Yes, I graduated from Youngstown State University," I replied. "Go Penguins," I added nervously. Really, Penguins? I thought.

Without acknowledging the Penguins comment, he got right to it, "I want to introduce you to your potential partner. Just so you are aware, if you accept this position, you will be the third teaching partner he has had this year. There are only five students in the classroom. You have a teaching partner, Cristian, and also a classroom assistant. I know that sounds easy, but they are quite the handful.

Five students? I could take attendance on one hand, I thought. And *three* adults? Remarkable ratio.

Just as that was sinking in, a tall guy wearing a powder blue oxford shirt, tie, and khaki pants with matching brown belt and shoes, walked in. He was holding a wooden clip board with what looked like point sheets. He never smiled.

I couldn't believe how much he looked like Malcom X, and suddenly I wondered if I was sitting in a Black History Month exhibition. It felt like I was sitting among greatness. I mean, it *was* February. February. And this is when I made the connection that I was going to be the third teacher for this classroom, and it's *February.*

"Hi," I said.

Without making eye contact he replied, "Hey."

"Cristian, let's have her take a look around and check out the classroom, shall we?" he asked.

He stood up and walked out.

Ok, good talk, I thought.

The three of us walked back past the now empty foyer and turned the corner.

"Ok, this is you," the principal said with a smirk. "Call me tomorrow if you still want the job," he said handing me his card. He turned and left.

What is it with these guys and their cards?

I stood in front of the door. 78. My first room number.

That's when the questions started. Are you our new teacher? How did you get so white? Is your pussy wet?

That last one caught me off guard.

I couldn't quite tell if they asked if I was their new teacher because they wanted a new teacher to help them learn, or if they simply wanted to know if I was their next target. I didn't respond.

I spent about a half hour in the room meeting the students and trying to get a feel for what the job was about. No academic work was being done. The students were popping in and out of their desks like popcorn in a machine. The classroom had a long closet on the inside wall. It ran about ten feet long and had openings on both ends. The closet seemed to be a time out area because students would pop out of their desk, say something inappropriate to another student, be sent to the closet for a bit, then released back to their desk.

It didn't seem to change their behavior because they went

right back to doing whatever it was, they were doing.

"Where are their books?" I asked Cristian.

"Books? he repeated back to me laughing sarcastically. "They destroyed most of them," he said.

I looked around the room. It looked like a bachelor pad for adolescent boys. Shoes and candy wrappers strewn about the floor. Worksheets covered the teacher's desk. The chalkboard featured colorful profanity. And the smell was almost unbearable. Though it didn't strike me initially, but in my effort to really understand the situation, it became clear that I was the only white person in the room.

A few male staff members popped their heads in to check out the new bait. They looked at me hard, gauging my skills and tenacity. I suddenly felt on display. I tried to play it cool when I met them. No mention of Penguins.

I went home that afternoon and thought long and hard about the job before me. The commute itself was going to be around 2 1/2 hours each day until we moved closer.

I couldn't stop thinking about how bad that classroom looked. It needed structure. Organization. Cleaned. *Books.*

I poured myself a glass of wine and looked through the portfolio that nobody would probably ever see. I reached into my pocket and pulled out the two business cards. Am I doing this?

Impossible odds. Unusual characters. Unpredictable situations. It's like I've been preparing my whole life for this job.

I called Mr James and said that I did, in fact, want the job.

"Excellent," he said. I'll send you a contract and let Human Resources know. "Oh," he went on, "one more thing. We offer graduate classes that are tailored to our program so we will need you to apply to graduate school right away and we can get you signed up for one of our behavior management classes."

"Grad school?" I asked. I felt distressed. I literally just finished the horse and pony show at Youngstown State.

Within a week's time, I was employed as a teacher/counselor, or TC, for five emotionally disturbed students in an alternative program based in Cleveland, and a graduate student at Kent State University.

From day one, the odds were against me. Five out of five students wanted me gone. It was undoubtedly their life mission to run me out. Bets as to how long I would last were secretly being made in nearby classrooms.

Within just a few hours of being on the job, I had been cursed at, called names that I didn't even understand, and threatened with physical harm. They ran out of the classroom, all of the time. One student in particular thought my name was White Ho-Ass Bitch.

In three days' time, I hadn't completed one lesson. The first time I handed a book to a student, he threw it right back at me, all the while spewing a sequence of profanity-laden prose that was as impressive and poetic as it was vulgar.

In debriefing with my colleagues at the end of those first few days, they shook their heads in disbelief of how absolutely terrible I was. They outlined my myriad of failures, followed by, it doesn't ever really get better.

Several more days passed with not much improvement. They were notorious runners. I learned quickly that it was a common practice to take their shoes as a deterrent to running. It was totally ineffective because I saw a shoe-less student jump out of the window and run into the snow-covered streets in just his socks. He couldn't care less about the shoes.

I was exhausted, frustrated, and completely in over my head. I spent my days getting my ass kicked and my nights drinking cheap wine and contemplating my options. I could quit. I wanted to quit. I was confident that I should quit.

Or I could give it more time.

I didn't know much, but I knew that I needed to get their behaviors under control. They needed incentives. And I needed to stop getting my ass kicked.

One night after some wine, I developed an elaborate plan to plaster all of the walls and ceiling with Velcro. I was going to buy yards of colorful felt and cut out cute little shapes and letters to form words of wisdom in hopes of inspiring the students to do something extraordinary with their lives. I would create a Word Wall with new vocabulary and samples of their own writing, and an Art Wall filled with their own creative versions of life. I could add endless games and activities and chart all of their academic and behavior progress using popsicle sticks.

Popsicle sticks and Velcro. That was my idea.

It was brilliant, I thought at the time. Maybe I'll even get nominated for Teacher of the Year.

I bought $250 worth of supplies, all money out of my own pocket. For the next four days, I hung Velcro and felt all over my classroom walls. I didn't even try to teach anything because I had a plan and I didn't have time to dodge books. I just needed it to work.

For four days they all watched me like a baby panda in the zoo. They were curious and bored. Two students got into a fist fight over what I was trying to do.

"Ms Ross, watcha doin?" an onlooker asked.

"It's a game asshole. You can't fucking see that? You're a stupid-ass mother fucker," said the student sitting next to him.

And so it began.

I remember feeling relieved the room got cleared that day because I needed to focus more now than ever. At the end of the day, I masterfully explained the plan to the three remaining students.

"It's simple," I told them. "You'll be rewarded for doing work and exhibiting good behavior." I explained how they can make their own pieces and move along from one popsicle stick to the next, earning all sorts of things. The final stick was a pizza party.

No reaction. None.

The next day I was out of the building for training and returned the following day to a pile of felt in the middle of the floor. What wasn't on the floor was drooping from the wall and ceiling. Popsicle sticks, cute little designs, all gone. They had even broken the one picture frame on my desk. It was a picture of my dog. You could still see pieces of glass on the floor. One desk was broken and pushed off into the corner. I scanned the room in disbelief.

One of the students had a popsicle stick in his mouth. It was the pizza party stick.

"Yo, Ms Ross," he said chomping on the stick, "looks like we get the pizza party."

Bastards, I thought.

It was a love/hate relationship the rest of the school year. I got hit with a chair. Pulled a back muscle breaking up a fight. I quit at least twice before being convinced to go back. Gradually, the running decreased but the aggressive behaviors continued. And, I was still a White Ho-Ass Bitch, which I tried desperately to shake early on.

"Why does it have to be racial?" I finally asked the young man one day. "Why can't I just be a Ho-Ass Bitch?" I was desperate for any amount of progress, no matter how small.

We took them to the gym all the time. I played basketball with them. I kept showing up, despite its many challenges. Every day I learned from them and they, in turn, let me help them learn. My teaching partner took me under his wing and helped me begin to understand the plight of young Black men. I read books. I immersed myself in Black History to become more culturally aware and responsive. I learned so much of the history I was taught in high school was implicitly biased. I felt betrayed in a sense; that I was brainwashed, and this upset me. I felt inadequately prepared for these conversations because I came in thinking I knew things, when in fact, I had so much more to learn. It's like when you learned Santa Claus was not real. It's devastating. How much time has been wasted believing in something that wasn't true?

Cristian and I would stay late into the school day talking. I asked questions and he gave it to me straight. We debriefed my performance each day. He broke down my actions in a play-by-play narrative. He brought things to my attention that I was completely unaware of.

You touch your hips a lot, he said. It makes you look nervous. And you never say 'No'. Are you afraid to say no? And when they swear at you, you back down.

It was all difficult to hear. But the conversations helped. I got better. I worked hard to not take things so personally. Let the insults roll right off me like a waterfall. To decrease my apparent hip-touching tics. But most importantly, I began to build the courage to say 'No'.

Over time, he softened, and the students noticed. We developed a relationship of mutual respect and collaboration. He came to my rescue more times than I can count. Took over when I couldn't. Taught me how to lick my wounds. I encouraged him to lean in more. Be engaged. It's an interesting thing, compassion, in an environment that may be void of empathy and caring relationships. It's hard to recognize, but it can sneak up on you when you least expect it.

I brought in books that they did not destroy. I taught lessons. We created reading groups and had group meetings. We slowly grew fond of each other and established some boundaries. I put masking tape on the floor around their desks to signify their personal space, and we made a rule that others could not violate that space unless invited in. This seemed to make them feel safer. I could feel the energy shifting. I learned how to de-escalate situations and needed rescued a lot less frequently. I gained confidence and learned how to say NO. Our classroom grew to 8. It seemed like each new student disrupted the pecking order and we had to start all over again. It was exhausting. And frustrating. But we slowly made progress. I held on until June, which felt a lot like holding onto a ski rope long after you lost your skis.

Out of pure stubbornness, I signed on for another year. I felt like we all had a lot more to learn, and I needed to fully understand the work I was charged with as an educator in that environment.

Everything I know about teaching I learned in that year and a half. They were hard lessons to learn, but I did gain some key insights. First, interventions should be research-based and not wine-inspired. Second, it was never about taking control. I mistakenly thought I needed to get the students under my control. All that did was create barriers and mistrust. As it turns out, shaping behaviors is far more beneficial than controlling them.

I also realized it is all about building relationships, being present, and meeting them where they are and slowly bringing them along. The students eventually settled down a bit because I spent the time to get to know them. Understand their situation and perspective. I showed my own vulnerability by asking questions and leaning into the discomfort of our differences. We pursued a common ground. We learned to name our feelings, acknowledge our failures, and embrace our successes. Sometimes I think I learned more from them than they did from me. Most importantly, I learned a good sense of humor goes a long way and that being called a Ho-Ass Bitch could potentially be a term of endearment.

17
Drinking with the Natives

It was June of 1996 and I just survived four grueling months of teaching students who had been kicked out of every school they had ever attended. It was a pilgrimage. My own personal journey toward progress. It seemed like every forward movement was sharply derailed by a sudden act of absurdity. Four months of enduring a barrage of psychological, emotional and, at times, physical pain.

I quit twice. Neither of them stuck, but being on the verge of quitting just about every day takes an emotional toll on you. It gets into your psyche and transcends rational thinking.

I couldn't help but think the daily punishment was a penance for my own youthful transgressions. For every time a student told me to fuck off, I remembered my own experiences in school, when I talked back to a teacher or pushed a kid out of frustration. It was payback, times ten. And every time one of my students had an explosive outburst I felt like a failure. That somehow it was my fault because I was doing it all wrong. I was on a runaway train and felt completely powerless.

There seemed to be so many differences between me and my students; crater-sized gaps in our knowledge and experiences. I never went hungry as a kid. We didn't have great food, and there was no structure or supervision with meals, but we had food to eat. These kids were hungry. Ravenous, even. I couldn't eat anything without them asking for some small part of it. Food was not just a motivator for them. It was primal. Some of our best moments in the classroom occurred during lunch, when their bellies were being filled.

I had very little supervision as a kid, and I often ran wild. But these students experienced real abandonment. Neglect, even. Needs unmet. Emotional growth stunted. Their lives were as unpredictable and chaotic as anything I had ever remotely experienced. Despite these differences, I connected with their struggles, which I felt deeply. I understood their anger and frustration, shared it almost, and empathized with the gaping hole it left after the dust settled. It resonated with me and I leaned in to understand it more.

Every minute of my day was consumed with motivating the students to engage in a positive way; to give learning a chance and break down the cultural barriers. The only thing they seemed curious about was me and my weird habits. What I ate. How I ate. My clothes. Why I say 'restroom' and not 'bathroom'. I spent hours trying to transfer that level of curiosity to learning. For every question they asked me, I asked them one back. I let them educate me on rap and pop culture. We shared musical interests and had long conversations about Tupac. We broke down his lyrics. I played Barbra Streisand for them and they fell on the floor holding their ears, screaming for me to turn her off. They were so dramatic about the whole thing. But I was willing to try anything to get them talking and listening to what others had to say.

On top of that, I had to navigate the unique alternative school culture. There was staff drama. Alliances. Unwritten codes of ethics and philosophies. The job didn't come with a manual on how to immerse yourself into this new culture. I had to figure it out. And do it while trying to dodge a fire hose.

Happy hours were a rite of passage. Required, even. If I was on a spiritual journey, happy hour was my Temple. It was a place to seek deeper meaning in the work, vent, swap war stories, laugh, cry, get encouragement, lick your wounds, and enjoy libations. I was an experienced drinker, but these people, they drank like professionals. Their tolerance and stamina were nothing short of Olympic-sized grandeur.

They drank with flair. And ordered two drinks at a time. A Long Island Iced Tea and Heineken. A Crown Royal and draft beer. Two tequilas. Two beers. It didn't matter as long as they came in twos. And they didn't just order a few drinks. Or stay a few hours. They consumed multiple drinks across several hours, often going well into the evening. Day after day. I was fascinated by them and thought, these are my people.

There's a theory about the kind of personalities that sit around a bar. And our crew had all of them. Quinn the quiet one, smiling at everyone, but talking to no one. Generally insecure in a crowded space, talking only to save face or order another round. Darryl the distracted game-watcher. Basketball. Football reruns from a decade ago. Golf, even. Anything to deflect the reality of the moment. Every now and then, placing a side bet on a game, a foul shot, or a subsidiary issue like who might go home with who at the end of the night.

Frankie the flirt. Always leaning in, whispering in an ear, touching a back. Occasionally winning bets for Darryl. Olly, the obnoxious one, always lighting short fuses around the room. Throwing jabs. Launching flamethrowers. Anything to ignite tempers and inspire controversy. Stopping only to reload or order another round. Finally, Harley the heavy drinker, the quintessential pace car who sets the tone early, heightens the flair, entertains the audience, and moderates any potential hazards.

They each were all of these things on any given night, and I watched them swerve in and out of them as the night went on.

They say that in extreme environments, people morph into something they are not, and begin to assimilate to the culture they are immersed in out of pure survival. Or, and this is quite possible, I already possessed some of those dysfunctional characteristics, and it was the intense environment that brought them out. Normalized them even. Either way, I got sucked in. Completely caught up in the debauchery, many times I found myself stumbling home around midnight.

It was a camaraderie like I had never experienced. The more terrible your day, typically, the more people showed up for you at happy hour. Perhaps that's one of the few benefits of working in an emotionally intense environment. We had long days filled with emotionally charged behaviors and uncomfortable situations. On occasion, students would become physically out of control and jeopardize their own safety, or the safety of others. In those instances, trained staff would intervene by physically restraining a student in order to secure the space. Always on our toes, we walked around in a constant state of readiness. Defense mechanisms were on high alert, always. Our fight or flight instincts ready to be deployed at a moment's notice.

The school building was large. It had to be in order to absorb their inordinate amount of energy. Students were spread out amongst ten classrooms, separated by age and/or grade levels. Class sizes topped out around ten students per classroom. Mine had five when I started. There was a Kindergarten through second grade room. A few third through fifth-grade rooms. A middle school room, which was mine. And a handful of high school rooms. There was also a main office, cafeteria, library, and incentive room where older students could play a game of foosball or just hang out.

The classrooms were close enough to offer assistance if needed, but far enough apart to feel isolated at times. For the most part, though, everyone had each other's backs. We were in it together. As long as you didn't violate any of the unwritten codes. For example, reporting an overly aggressive restraint or breaking an alliance in some way could potentially wreak havoc. You might be left alone in a hostile room to fend for yourself. Calls for help might go unanswered, or they may be slow to respond. This was their territory. They made the rules. They were the natives and I was a newbie; an outsider. I had zero clout and took a lot of shit for my mistakes.

"Seriously, Diane," Harley slurred one late afternoon, "What were you thinking?"

"He literally undressed right in front of you!" Olly shouted from the bar. Laughter erupted.

Olly was one of two support staff members, so he was always in and out of all the classrooms, assisting as needed. As such, he had all the scoop of the day. And in this case, he was right.

*

Earlier in the day, one of my students did not earn the regularly scheduled gym time. As a result, he had to stay back in the classroom. I elected to stay with him so I could work on some lesson plans. It was just the two of us in the room.

He was seated in the row closest to my desk. I can't use the excuse that he wasn't in my line of sight, because I could see him crystal clear. Pre-occupied with my lessons, I never saw him take his shoes and socks off. But in my defense, it wasn't unusual for students to be barefoot. When I arrived on the job, it was common practice to confiscate shoes if a student was considered a flight risk. It also added a little extra incentive for them to behave appropriately to earn them back. Once a student lost his shoes, sometimes they either didn't have socks on to start with, or they were filled with holes so to save from embarrassment, they took them off too.

I saw him barefoot and thought, well he's just getting comfortable. Whatever.

Before I knew what happened, he stood up, took his shirt off and walked over to my desk and picked up an air freshener I had sitting on the corner. I watched him take the lid off and wipe the gel all over his chest and under his armpits.

"Ohhhhhh, this smells so good. Smell me now," he said wiping it all over his neck and stomach.

I immediately instructed him to put the air freshener back on my desk and put his shirt on, in that order. I'm not sure what that says about my priorities, but Lord knows that room needed some air freshener.

He completely ignored both requests and continued scooping out the air freshener gel, wiping it all over his face and behind his ears. He wandered around a bit, and that little bit of movement caused his saggy pants to droop even more, until they finally hung around his knees. With his shoes and socks already off, he simply stepped right out of them. It all happened so quickly.

For some reason, I was still sitting in my desk and only when I stood up, did the reality of the situation become clear. He was standing in the middle of the classroom, covered in purple air freshener gel, completely naked, except for his dingy boxer shorts.

Well shit, I thought.

I started to walk toward the door, but he cut me off at the path. And that's when I saw the look in his eyes shift. It wasn't about the air freshener any more, though he did smell pleasant. I knew I needed to get to the door before it became a weird sexual encounter, though I suspect it had already come to that.

"Ok," I said. "Here's what's going to happen. You're going to hurry up and put your clothes back on because there is still ten minutes left of gym time and I'm going to let you go," I conceded. But trying to save face, "Clearly you need to burn off some energy and I'd like to see you do that in a healthy way," I said to make myself feel better.

But it didn't matter, because in the midst of negotiating the situation, Olly walked in and, though caught off guard, immediately offered assistance.

I wasn't completely surprised that I got called into the principal's office after school to answer some questions. Namely, how did it come to be that a support staff member walked into your classroom and saw an almost naked student covered in purple air freshener gel standing in the middle of the room, doing what appears to be, blocking you from exiting?

Fair question, I thought.

It was pointed out to me that I had a variety of options to explore prior to him getting down to his boxer shorts. Once Mr

Johnson, the principal, presented these options out loud, of course, they made perfectly good sense to me. But how do you come up with the options in the first place, right? I mean, that is half the battle. Had I come up with options, I certainly would have tried each and every one of them. I mean, if everyone knew all of the available options in the exact moment they needed them, well then, everyone would be making much better decisions with their lives.

To be honest, I don't know if it was a lack of options or not fully understanding the scope of all possible outcomes in the situation; but either way, in the eyes of many, I had failed. And I heard about it for several hours later that day at the bar.

A few weeks later, Mr Johnson came by the classroom and explained to me that part of the alternative school program included therapeutic field trips, and he asked when we would be taking our students on one.

"Therapeutic what kind of trips?" I asked.

"Field trips," he replied.

I looked at him, then back into the classroom, where two students were chasing a third around the reading table. One of them farted so loud it stopped everyone in their tracks, and they all fell to the floor laughing.

I looked back at Mr Johnson, "Like, out of the building kind of field trip?"

"Uh huh. Let me know when you want to sign the van out," he said walking away.

I quickly asked Cristian if we could stall. "We don't have a new classroom assistant for Sean yet. So, it's a two to six ratio, with Sean. We aren't ready," I told him.

Sean was so volatile that he required his own aide. But the aide recently left to play for an international basketball team.

180

Sean had been enjoying his new freedom, to say the least.

"You are never really ready," he said. "You just go and whatever happens, happens. If he says we gotta go, we gotta go," he finished. After a long pause, "Personally, I hate it."

A week later, I was standing in the office signing out the van while Cristian loaded up the supplies. We had a cooler, charcoal, and a few frisbees and footballs. I even prepared some team building activities. I walked outside to the chaos of the students running around with excitement and Cristian already looking annoyed. The program mandated we wear ID badges anytime we left the building with the students. But in that moment, I knew there wasn't an ID badge big enough to help me handle this situation.

As soon as I opened the van, they all rushed in, fighting over seats and yelling names of who they did and did not want to sit next to. He smells. He doesn't ever shut up. He's trifling.

I started opening the passenger side door and Cristian looked at me and said, "Yea, hey, you'll have to drive because I — well, I don't actually have a driver's license."

"What?" I asked.

"Well, I do have one, but due to some unfortunate circumstances, it's actually suspended," he said. "I thought we talked about this," he said opening the passenger side door for himself.

Has anyone seen my car? I thought. I was notoriously a bad driver. My rearview mirror was duck taped onto the car because of an unfortunate ATM incident the week before. And a few weeks before that, I pulled away from the gas pump, with the hose still attached to my car.

"No, I'm pretty sure I would remember that I was going to be responsible for the lives of six young people today," I said furiously.

I crawled into the driver's seat and put my seatbelt on. I was the lone white person in the car. The minority in the situation. I thought about it for a second. Looked around. They didn't seem to mind one bit. Perhaps to them, we were going somewhere. To this day, I can't say for sure what they thought, if it even mattered to them. But in that moment, I knew we had to get moving before they all lost their shit. I hollered back for everyone else to buckle up. No sooner did I pull out onto the street the first fight erupted. We stopped, re-arranged some seats, and continued on. As the noise got louder in the back seat, Cristian turned up the radio. Classical music. I didn't see that coming.

Cristian was notoriously difficult to work with. His interpersonal antics were legendary around the building. It's safe to say that people weren't lining up to work with him. He was intense, and always trying to gain greater insight into my psyche as a way to establish control over how much he would or would not trust me. He used to play a game called 'What's your favorite?' At first, I didn't understand the point. But he would randomly ask me a relatively benign question like, "What's your favorite magazine?" I don't know, I'd say. Smithsonian. Or Backpacker.

"Ok," he would say. "Based on that, I can infer you like history, art and culture, the outdoors, and hiking. Which also tells me you are active, curious, and that you like to read and learn new things." Twenty minutes of him telling me what I liked or didn't like based on my magazine selection, or whatever I listed as my 'favorite.' He wasn't entirely off, but it became a bit invasive after a while. I felt like he was always studying me, which was weird because I didn't think I was that interesting.

I say all of that to say, I suspect the classical music was a way to throw me off his scent; a way for him to keep me on my toes and avoid predictability. Kind of like forgetting to tell me he didn't have a driver's license until we were ready to pull out of the parking lot.

About twenty minutes later we rolled into the park. We unloaded everything and the students took off running like a group of puppies who've never seen grass. Their pure joy and excitement also caught me off guard. I wasn't expecting them to get so excited about being outside. As a kid, I was always outside, riding my bike, or playing in the woods. My dad took me camping and waterskiing regularly. I was so busy trying to manage the classroom, that it never occurred to me that my students didn't always have those kinds of opportunities to get out into open spaces. Watching them run around in the grassy field brought me a lot of joy, and I was immediately glad we made the trip happen.

Cristian fired up the grill and I occupied the students with games. We had foot races, played tag, laughed, and had a genuinely fun time. After we ate, the students asked me twenty questions about where I grew up, why didn't I have kids, how did I come to be their teacher, and did I think they were all crazy.

The spontaneous back and forth exchanges flowed easily and we connected in a way that made it clear we were turning a corner. I liked their questions and they cared about my answers. We were meeting in the middle. A relationship was forming. Only when I reflect on that moment do I realize that it was authentic engagement. I could never write a lesson plan for that moment. It just happened organically. A curiosity emerged in them and the engagement seemed worth their time and energy. They saw, potentially, a return on their investment. It was one of those moments when I knew I was doing exactly what I was meant to do in life.

It got late in the day, so we packed up the van, and feeling more accomplished than when I woke up that morning, I confidently jumped into the driver's seat and pulled out. Cristian and I were navigating the Shaker Heights neighborhood streets to classical music, deep in conversation, when an enormous commotion erupted from the back. We heard the sound of the van door opening, followed by loud screams. I looked back and saw Sean jumping out. I just remember seeing the back of his baseball cap and a flailing jacket in the wind. The other students went absolutely ballistic.

"Holy Shit! What the fuck is he doing? He's going to get hit by a car! That's just stupid," I heard from the back.

"Shit, more room for us," Jamal said taking Sean's window seat.

"We got a jumper," Cristian said calmly. "Pull over so we can assess the situation."

"A jumper?" I screamed. "Assess the situation?" I went on. WE JUST LOST A KID!" I shouted as I pulled over to the side of the road. I immediately put my hazards on.

Shit, this is definitely my last day. I'm going to get fired. Who jumps out of a moving vehicle traveling 25 MPH down the road? He couldn't wait until I hit a stop sign? I was expecting the rest of the students to revolt as well. I thought if one went, there were sure to be others. So, while Cristian chased down the jumper, I quickly engaged the others. I asked them what happened. If they were OK. Did they have fun at the park? Whatever I could think of to keep them talking, and in the vehicle.

Cristian came back empty handed. "Well, he doesn't live around here so nowhere for him to go but back to the school," he said calmly.

He was right. That's where we found him.

"We have to tell Mr Johnson," I said. "Like, that's not normal, jumping out of a moving van," I continued.

"Six out, six back," Cristian said. "It's done. Let's move on."

I didn't feel entirely comfortable with the decision, but it made sense to me in the moment. I was exhausted. I needed to get them on their bus home and prepare for the next day. Alliance kept. Check. No unwritten codes broken. Also check.

A few hours after the buses pulled out, we tucked ourselves into a small corner at the neighborhood bar to process the day. I watched Cristian guzzle a handful of Long Island Iced Teas and a half dozen Heinekens. A few drinks turned into a dozen and I got loose with my questions.

Why don't you drive? What's with all your 'favorite' questions? How do I break through? What's wrong with these kids? When does it all start to make sense? His answers swirled around the mix of chatter floating from across the room.

"With all your students gone today, it was so quiet we took a three-hour lunch," Olly jabbed from his table across the room. "I've never been so bored," he hollered. Our students were notoriously difficult, and we needed his assistance far more than Cristian's pride would have liked.

"Can you take them on a field trip every week?" Olly shouted again. The entire bar erupted in laughter.

Usually that would incite Cristian to get up and banter

with him for a while, maybe call him out on some hidden inadequacy that would ultimately send Olly home with his tail between his legs. Olly was always getting between us, and their bantering was exhausting. But not today.

He shook his head laughing and continued to drink his Heineken.

"I don't drive because I lost my license and I haven't quite gotten around to getting it back," he said finally. He then rambled on about a series of what appeared to be inconsequential traffic violations, that to me, seemed like something I would shrug off. But for him, the points accrued and his patience for it diminished, and he landed on the conclusion that public transportation was his best option.

"Seems trivial," I said naively.

He laughed at the joke I didn't realize I made. "Trivial." he said with that familiar you have so much to learn tone.

I could see him dancing around my statement.

"There's nothing trivial about being Black and driving a car," he said finally.

I had seen the news and heard stories, so I instantly knew what he was talking about. It was spring of 1996 and it had been five years since Rodney King famously survived a brutal beating at the hands of the Los Angeles Police Department. Despite the widely seen disturbing video, the officers were acquitted of police brutality, which sparked riots across Los Angeles that lasted for days.

Despite my naive comment, I understood these cultural disparities on a conceptual level. But I had never met anyone who went to the lengths he did to avoid driving. With three small kids at home, he could have easily given in and towed the line. But he dug his heels in, I suspect, out of pure principle. It wasn't fear that kept him out of the driver's seat, necessarily; but rather, it was a giant fuck you to the world. I listened intently to his story and respected that fact.

Unaware of it at the time, that conversation sparked a year-long carpooling adventure; whereby that following school year, I picked him up every morning from his house. We drove into work together. Sometimes we planned the day. Other times, he slept. But we always drove in together. Despite the scandalous rumors, Cristian and I turned his mission of staying out of the driver's seat into something far more special. A true partnership.

Though our colleagues may have suspected something else entirely, we left the bar together that night, and I dropped him off at the bus stop. Before he got out of the car, he looked back at me and said, "The kids are the way they are because they are dist-tuuur-bed." He laid out 'disturbed' with the kind of southern drawl that left a word hanging in the air like an engine-less plane about to crash-land.

After the van incident, they started bringing in applicants for Sean's classroom assistant position. One trickled in every few days, took a look around, spent some time in the room, and we never saw him again. Low pay. Difficult work. And it's not for everyone.

One day a clean-cut looking young guy named Kevin walked in. He was African American, and probably in his early twenties. He topped out at 5'7", not much taller than Sean. He had a very distinctive soprano-type voice and a meekness to him. We interviewed him over the course of a few different visits. He seemed interested in the work and I saw some goodness in him. He was genuine. Outwardly caring. I thought he could bring a little positivity to the classroom. Christian was not a fan. I presume he didn't care for Kevin because he appeared 'soft' and lacked the bravado that was pervasive among the male staff throughout the building. It's true, Kevin wasn't going to be invited to the private Saturday morning basketball games. Personally, Kevin's personality was refreshing, and ultimately it was my decision. Plus, we were desperate for some extra hands, so we brought him on.

It only took a few days for the students to find his weak spot. I initially enjoyed the reprieve of disparaging remarks. For once, they weren't aimed at me. Kevin's entrance in the room elevated everyone up in the pecking order, including me. The students even began to lean on me a little more. I was familiar to them. A known entity. We suddenly had an alliance.

Despite the calmness for me, the situation deteriorated quickly. I tried to mediate their differences and help Kevin gain some confidence. I shared all the strategies that I found to be helpful. Don't take things personally. Get to know them more. Be creative. Work with what little they give you in return. Don't turn your back on them. Thwart any potential disasters. He tried so hard to be firm, fit in, and do his job. But the students were relentless. "Did you wipe your ass?" they would ask when he returned from the restroom. "What took so long? Were you jacking off?"

And they would roll on with that for a while, asking him all sorts of wildly inappropriate questions about his hypothetical masturbation habits in public restrooms.

On one particularly rough day, we had four students in time out. The time out area in our classroom was a long ten-foot closet area that opened on both ends. Students often used the space to cool off or just take some time away from the group. Sometimes a student would ask to take space, or a staff member might suggest they take a few minutes, or, in this case, students were escorted to the space due to out of control behaviors. If there were multiple students in the space, staff usually flanked the ends and released students back to their desks when they were more in control of their behavior.

In this event, we had four students in the closet area, and two remaining at their seat. Cristian was sitting in a chair at the front end of the closet, calculating behavior point sheets on his clipboard, and tuning out the chaos. Each student had their own point sheet broken up into categories like peer interaction, work completion, and following directions. In addition to these general behaviors, they each also had individualized goals.

Sean, for example, might be working on reducing his aggressive behaviors; while Jamal might have a goal to reduce inappropriate language. Students were rated twice a day, in the morning, and again in the afternoon. So, essentially if they messed up in the morning, they still had an opportunity to salvage their day in the afternoon. Their points determined what level of privileges they were on. More points meant more privileges. And the opposite was true. Fighting or seriously aggressive behavior put you on restriction and you had to earn your way back on level. The entire classroom management system relied on these points, so calculating them on time was important work.

I remained out in the common area with the other two at their desk, teaching an academic lesson. Kevin was in the closet area and floated in and out of my view. The students in the time out area started to get louder and I could hear them really taunting Kevin. At first, Kevin used his sweet voice to ask them to stop. The sweet voice turned to desperation. Somewhere in there I missed panic and fear. And I definitely missed the sound of the fuse sizzling away inside of him.

189

Every now and then I would walk over to the closet and give him a nod, encourage him to keep at it, suggest he stay more on the outside of the space. Then I'd return back to my lesson. But he kept floating inward trying to interact with the students. I'm just trying to calm them down, he said. Not realizing he was the bait. I finally decided to stay over near the rear opening of the closet. Cristian was still sitting at the front entrance, now holding a student's arm with one hand and calculating his points with the other. Every now and then the student would lunge at Kevin, and Cristian would pull him back.

I was slowly trying to get students back to their seats. Bribing them essentially. No takers. What was happening in the time out area was far more exciting than anything I could offer them on the outside. And they just continued to feed off each other, escalating exponentially with each new outrageous taunt.

Seconds turned to minutes, and the taunting turned to threats. "Why's your voice so high? Did someone cut your balls off?" Jamal asked leading the charge. He got right in Kevin's face, "I can deepen your voice for you, you punk ass bitch." He was nose-to-nose with him, spitting out nonsensical put-downs. "I bet your farts are so high pitched they hurt your dog's ears." And, "You probably hang from your balls at night, you, crazy bat-shit, high pitched, high-water pant wearing bat wannabe!"

I finally stepped in to intervene. I tried to separate the two, but Kevin wasn't backing down. I even reminded him, in that moment, that he was the adult in the situation. But it was too late. Kevin leaned in over me, pointing at Jamal's face; and, in an effort to retaliate, Jamal leaned back in over me pointing at Kevin's face. I was suddenly sandwiched between the two.

I looked over at Cristian, who finally stood up and slowly put down his clipboard. He used his pointer finger to push up his glasses and shook his head in irritation. By the time he eased into the tangled mess, it was all four students against Kevin, circling him like lions about to pounce on their prey. Completely overwhelmed, I stepped back just in time to see Kevin explode in a boisterous tirade.

"You're fucking crazy! What the fuck is wrong with you?" He screamed in Jamal's face. And finally, "You're the punk-ass N — bitch!"

That's when Jamal knew he'd won. He flipped Kevin's switch and he was beaming with pride. He stepped back to enjoy the show.

Kevin threatened each and every one of us, telling us we were all fucking crazy and that he had hoped we all went to hell. He pushed his way out of the closet area and leaped over Cristian's chair, shredding the crotch of his pants. The students went absolutely nuts over this, falling to the floor with laughter. We could hear him swearing all the way down the hallway, calling everyone a mother fucker and telling everyone to go to hell, including Mr Johnson, who happened to be coming into the building when he was running out.

By the time Mr Johnson made it to our classroom to check on the situation, the students had returned to their desks and were eerily calm. They had completely exhausted themselves and the look of satisfaction on their faces was alarming. Six out of six students said he was a terrible assistant and deserved to be fired for what he did to Jamal.

Mr Johnson agreed right there on the spot. And Cristian did not disagree.

I mean, for sure the students provoked him in that situation, and they should have all been placed on restriction.

It was brutal and I felt terrible for the guy. But at the end of the day, Kevin was the adult and, consequently, held to a higher standard.

I didn't challenge the decision. Alliance kept. Check. No unwritten codes violated. Also Check.

Mr Johnson showed up to happy hour later that day. He was the pace car. His re-enactment of Kevin running out of the building was nothing short of pure theatrical genius. Cristian highlighted the crotch-shredding moment, and because I have a knack for remembering detailed put-downs, apparently, I recalled the final blow to Kevin's ego. Hanging from the balls bat wannabe. Say what you want, that was creative as hell. Wildly inappropriate, of course, but creative.

Not long after that, I sat next to the keg of beer at the end-of-the-year party in June, playing a little game called Drink Master, which is essentially me pouring the beer for people and also trying to match the drink for drink pace of my colleagues, I thought about some things.

First, survival is relative. And it comes at a cost. Because in order to survive you have to change in some dramatic way. It's like grabbing the last life vest on a sinking ship. In your effort to survive, you have to unfortunately watch others drown. It changes you. And it's not something you ever forget.

For four months I watched Cristian work the classroom like a master magician, a true sleight-of-hand artist, with suave movements that kept us in the game. I envied his style and command of the room. I tried to do what he did, word for word, and sometimes action for action. But the outcomes were always vastly different. I was not him, in any way. While they genuinely listened to him, I often felt like they only listened to me because of him.

Over time, though, I learned how to play my own game.

Find my stride. Because the more you try to ignore or outrun race and culture, the further away you get from a common goal. The only way to real change is to lean in wholeheartedly and embrace change. And my survival in the classroom depended on that.

Second, it's not always about black and white. Sometimes, you need to become comfortable with grey. In optimal situations, right is right and wrong is wrong. But what about those murky situations? Are you willing to lose everything to be right? It wouldn't have served any real purpose to tell the principal we had a student jump out of a moving van. But it made all the difference that I didn't tell the principal we had a student jump out of a moving van.

Finally, the connections you make with others are valuable, whether you choose to keep them or not. And the more you nurture them, the deeper they become. Whether they remain strong or end poorly, they all serve a purpose, and bring you along to the place where you need to be.

If I really think about it, my dad taught me early on the value of good interpersonal connections. When I was a kid, we would be out somewhere, and he would run into a guy I never met before. I'd watch him leaning in, talking, laughing, listening intently; and I'd think, who is this guy? They looked like best friends the way they carried on.

"No, I just met him," my dad would later tell me. "Seems like he might be kind of goofy," he went on, "but he did have some interesting perspectives on things."

"If he's goofy, why did you talk to him so long?" I asked.

"Listen kid, if you think I have my shit together, you are sorely mistaken. You don't think there are people out there who think I'm goofy as hell? I'm just saying, don't get hung up on people's differences or quirks because you might lose out on a good friend down the road. You give everyone a fair shake, you hear me?" he asked making sure his point landed. "And only then do you move along if you still can't see making it work," he finished.

My dad has an interesting way of describing people. He puts them into three distinct categories: straight shooter, goofy, and pretty fucked up. He seems to find value in all of them, and would never throw someone to the curb who was 'kind of goofy.' In fact, those are qualities he is most attracted to. For years, one of his best friends was a guy he only referred to as "my dumpster diving buddy". You would think a guy who dives in dumpsters regularly falls in the pretty fucked up category, but not according to my dad. On the contrary, a person who doesn't appreciate a good piece of junk and thinks they are too good for such things; well, he's likely to say they are pretty fucked up.

It's a lesson that stuck with me. As I sat there next to the keg drinking my beer, looking around at the motley cast of characters, I saw the full spectrum of straight shooters, goofballs, and pretty fucked up people. In some way or another, each played a role in helping me cross the finish line. Lasting relationships or not, and whether it was through sound advice or biting sarcasm, they each had a profound impact on my development and pushed me to become a better person and teacher. Education programs, books, and professional development has its place, for sure. They certainly provide a framework and offer guiding principles on diversity in education. But for me, there's no better way to immerse yourself in a new culture than drinking with the natives.

18
On Finding Peace in Outhouses

Five years later, I found myself sitting on the dirt floor of an African hut, amidst a dozen buckets of varying sizes, shapes, and colors. I contemplated which one I would, inevitably, use the most. Why so many? I wondered. A bucket is a bucket. Used universally. It seems so simple, I thought to myself as I meticulous lined them up according to size. Of all the things I read about Africa prior to becoming a Peace Corps Volunteer and moving here, buckets never came up. But each one of them, as it turns out, serves its own purpose — to hold and transport water, do dishes, laundry, act as a substitute bathroom, and the largest of the bunch, serves as a full-on bathtub.

Only later did I learn they could take on other functions too. Like a step stool, animal catcher, weapon, and in an absolute pinch, a pillow. Each, invariably, tells an authentic African story.

I randomly picked one up, turned it around, and curiously rubbed my unclean hands around its rim. It came with a lid. I turned it over and began using it as a drum. Anything to pass the time.

A few days earlier, a beautiful African woman handed me the same bucket and said, "You'll need this for pee." She shoved it into my hands like it was the last life jacket and we were about to get on a partially floating boat.

"I'm sorry, for what?" I asked, hesitantly taking it from her hands.

"You go to bed at dark and need to pee in the night," she said matter of factly. "And no go to the outhouse at night. Dangerous for you," she added.

"Are people being murdered in outhouses?" I asked.

"Just take," she finished abruptly and walked off.

Since there were no corners in my one-room rondavel hut, I placed the now-identified pee bucket at the foot of my bed, and to the left of the front door. To be clear, it was the only door. But I thought the pee bucket was a nice bit of welcome for visitors. As if to say, it's been a long journey for you; please, if you must, here is a bucket to pee in. If I learned anything in my short time in Africa, it was to have some common courtesy and genuine hospitality. Mind you, it didn't occur to me to put a curtain up or anything. Just a bucket out in the open. My dad would be proud, I thought.

Suddenly, I had the urge to pee. I pulled up my loosely tied skirt and hovered over the bucket. Feeling relieved, I unanimously decided that *this* is the bucket I will use the most.

I covered my urine and looked around at my new home for the next two years. Or, for at least however long I could possibly stand it.

The newly constructed hut donned a beautifully crafted thatched roof. It sheltered me from the elements, while simultaneously housing families of insects and rodents. A dozen buckets, I need. But a net to keep African bugs the size of Mt. Kilimanjaro from falling on me while I sleep? No, you'll be fine, they said.

I had a small kitchen table in the center of the hut,

accompanied by two wooden chairs.

A lone gas lantern set on the table. My only light source. My kitchen utensils cluttered the top of a blue and white metal dry sink along the far-left wall. And just beyond that, A propane stove sat on a second wooden table. I had one large kettle for boiling water. And one pan for cooking. To round out the hut, a single bed lay off to the right, under the only window. The neck of my acoustic guitar, a gift from my teaching colleagues before I left for Africa, rested peacefully on my pillow. The setup seemed surprisingly functional in spite of not having any electricity or running water.

Draping over the table was a colorful tablecloth, which I bought on a trip into town a month earlier. I desperately purchased it in the midst of a chaotic shopping spree because I, mistakenly, thought it was a skirt. It became apparent very early on that I failed to fully understand the directive noted in the 'Before you Leave for Africa as a United States Peace Corps Volunteer' paperwork, in all capitalized, bold, underscored, 14 font, italicized print, ***SKIRTS FOR WOMEN ARE REQUIRED.***

I interpreted that to mean, skirts are strongly suggested and most likely meant for all the other girls on this journey. Having never been accustomed to wearing a skirt; nor, by the way, anyone ever encouraging or suggesting I might try a skirt, or even the simple fact that in my entire life, I have never worn a skirt; it therefor did not occur to me that I should, in fact, pack a skirt.

"Oh my God, Diane," a fellow volunteer said on our second day in Africa. "You didn't bring any skirts?" she asked folding her 100th skirt and placing it into the drawer of the makeshift dresser of our dorm.

Dorm living was also something I had never experienced. At 28 and newly divorced, for the past five years I lived in a three-bedroom, two bath house on a corner lot in the suburbs. With a husband and Labrador retriever. And prior to that, I stayed in the upstairs apartment above my father while working my way through college. I assumed dorm life consisted of girls laying around in pajamas on each other beds talking girl stuff, of which I couldn't be bothered. It turns out I assumed correctly, as that is what mostly occurred. I was lucky though, because my two roommates for Africa School were a perfect match for me. Both were mid-westerners, funny, laid back, and messy. More importantly, they also recognized and embraced the absurdity of the situation we found ourselves in.

I didn't enroll in Africa School like one might enroll in community college. It was more like the Red Cross met the CIA and they conceived a boot camp child. Immediately upon arrival, we were shuttled from the airport in Johannesburg to a secure compound in Lesotho, Africa. There, we endured six weeks of intense language and culture training. Twenty-four hours a day. Seven days a week. It was designed to teach us how to not offend the native people. And how to not get sick and die in Africa. Or murdered. There was definitely an emphasis on not getting murdered. During this time, they tested our aptitude, attitude, and overall psychological fitness.

"I want to be dropped off by a helicopter in the middle of nowhere," I told them in one interview about my upcoming full-time placement in country.

They stared at me, perplexed, and scribbled notes onto a piece of paper attached to a clipboard.

I'm sure they sensed, accurately, that whatever handful of

skills I was acquiring in training did not match the level of isolation I was requesting.

I stumbled through Africa School much like I did high school. I followed the rules just enough to not get kicked out. I made it to the finish line, but I didn't excel in any way. I lingered in the basic level language class, hanging onto phrases such as, 'I need help,' 'I'm sick,' 'Where is the hospital?' 'Leave me alone,' and my favorite, 'I am lost.' I watched my peers diligently studying and climbing to the top of their respective groups. Sometimes I jumped up with them just to play around, but my comfort level was definitely in the 'I need the bathroom' group. I envied their enthusiasm and selfless commitment to the cause. I could tell they were destined for great volunteer work.

I, on the other hand, was taking it all one day at a time. I walked around wondering, "Is today the day I pack up and go home?" I was certainly motivated to learn the basic necessities of daily African life, and fully prepared to embrace all that came with it. But I wasn't trying to learn how to request a particular food seasoning or have a statue named after me. I just wasn't that ambitious. Consequently, by the end of Africa School, I understood just enough to get into trouble, but not nearly enough to find my way out of it. I was relatively confident that as long as I didn't veer too far off the beaten path, I would probably be ok. Or not. One never really knows in Africa.

*

Whatever formula they used to derive my placement, I ended up sitting in a hut stationed squarely on top of a hill overlooking the rural village of Thaba-Tseka, one of ten districts in Lesotho, a land-locked country surrounded entirely by South Africa. Lesotho is one of the highest countries in the world; whereby, the entire country lies above 1,000 meters, or 3,281 feet in elevation. It's also one of the least known countries in the world.

My hut was a treacherous six-hour drive back to the capital city and Peace Corps compound. It would take a couple of days to drive back to the Johannesburg airport, by private car of course; or, a week, if you are relying on the public taxi service. And it sat roughly 8,000 long miles away from my hometown of Cortland, Ohio, and all things familiar.

*

I had only been divorced for a few months when I began packing for this journey. Material things like couches, televisions, and end tables served no purpose for me any more so I gave them all a way. Even my car, which was fairly new. I called my ex-husband one morning and said he could have the car, which I acquired in the divorce settlement. He was surprised but showed up later that night to claim it. It was a short conversation.

"Do you know what you're doing?" he asked.

"Not really," I answered.

"I can't believe you're giving everything up," he said looking around at my temporary living conditions — an old apartment building off a very busy street in the city. "Are you staying here?" he asked. Still looking around the dark parking lot trying to make sense of it all. "It doesn't even look safe," he finished.

"I have been, and probably not," I answered.

I handed him the keys. "I'm — I'm just — sorry," I stammered.

*

My divorce caught a lot of people off guard, for sure. And to the surprise of many, including myself, I came out as gay. Nothing screams change of pace like getting a divorce, coming out gay, giving all of your possessions away, and quitting your job to become a Peace Corps Volunteer in Africa. Those four things happened, precisely, in that order. Although, some could argue about number's one and two —* which came first, the chicken or the egg? Either way, all of those things required a fair amount of explanation. So, I did what made sense to me at the time. I jumped on the first plane to Africa with a backpack and one large duffle bag, neither of which contained skirts, and embarked on a life-changing journey.

*

The truth is, I had started making plans to join the Peace Corps about half-way through college. I desperately wanted to be part of something bigger; to contribute to the greater good of humankind in some meaningful way. Cheesy, I know. But a marriage proposal distracted me and changed the trajectory of my life. I have never regretted that sidestep, mostly because the experiences you have define you, and shape who you ultimately become. To that end, it didn't take long for me to re-focus on the Peace Corps once the marriage dissolved. Much like a hound on a scent, I could not be deterred.

As I sat in my hut, I tried to absorb all that I had been through. An unorthodox upbringing. A very difficult college experience. A wild teaching gig. Divorce. Coming out. And, most recently, Africa School. But I had a distinct feeling that living in Africa was going to be the beginning of a new kind of journey me.

The door of my hut was the gateway to another world. Just outside, a large garden overlooked the entire village. Hanging above that, there were strings of clothes lines. Upon being dropped off earlier in the day, I was welcomed not only by my host family, but also by a very large hanging bath towel sporting a colorful graphic of a naked woman with incredibly large boobs. I wasn't offended necessarily, given my new-found appreciation for women, but the brightly colored X-rated image was shocking and stood out against the otherwise drab backdrop of a poor African village. It just seemed out of place; but also, highlighted the juxtaposition of things that I would ultimately come to love most about Africa.

Fifty steps from my door sat a newly constructed tin outhouse with my name on it. Literally, there was a giant sign posted on the door that read "For Only Lerato". Lerato is an African name that was bestowed upon me during Africa School. It means Love. Hysterical, I thought. I was newly divorced and just left behind a trail of destruction and failed relationships. I was practically raised by wolves and had no real understanding of the word. And after a few short weeks of being in Africa, a team of native Basotho women unanimously decided that my name should represent all things related to love.

There was no way I could live up to that expectation.

I was just about to ask for another name when one of the

ladies said, "You laugh a lot, and it is like love."

Oh. OK. That makes way more sense, I thought.

So, I kept Lerato.

To be honest, I didn't quite understand, or fundamentally *know*, Love. Do you *learn* how to love? Does it come naturally? Are passion and love the same thing? What about sex and love? Is love destined only for relationships, or can it transcend human connection? Can you fail at it, but then find it again later? I had so many questions.

What I did know, was that when it came to love, I felt a lot like a kid standing behind a glass case at the candy counter. Surveying the lot. Drooling at the mouth. Too short to reach over the counter. Too young to understand the process. I could see it. The one I wanted. Everyone around me got the piece they wanted. But mine sat just outside of my grasp, and I was unable to find the words to ask for it.

They say it always starts with the parents. And having parents who decidedly raised their children to roam free suggests they organically show their love and affection in unique ways. Right? I mean that makes sense. But it could be argued from both perspectives. One. They didn't love you enough to carefully watch every move you made, ensuring you never felt discomfort or got into trouble. Or, two. They loved you *so* much that they wanted you to experience life in its purist form, at the risk of pain and disappointment. There's a third, I suppose. That they were so incredibly indifferent that parenting just didn't occur to them.

But as a kid and young adult, you can't rationalize those arguments. And, to be fair, it's really not your job as a kid to go around trying to rationalize things and figure out how love works. So, you fumble around in the dark, building walls around yourself to keep people out. It's just easier that way. But you can only stifle those feelings for so long before they take on a life of their own. Become an obstacle. A barrier to the things you want,` or need. Explosive, even. Or you escape altogether, move to Africa, and get an outhouse of your own. A place to contemplate deep questions when you have no other sources of entertainment.

Having been in Thaba-Tseka less than 24 hours, I sat on the floor in the middle of my hut, trying hard to filter my thoughts. How long can I go without a shower? Where can I find a cold beer? The hair on my legs seems eager to come out. What am I even going to *do* here? Jesus, it smells bad.

I tried to embrace the profound quiet and give myself permission to feel. It was an entirely new concept. *Feeling.* I had shut that down a long time ago. But the thing about divorce is that it doesn't kill you. At least not in the literal sense. It can certainly make you *feel* like you're dying. It takes you right to the edge. Suffocates you. Leaves you breathless and gasping for air. Blankness carves out space in your chest, leaving a gaping hole where your heart used to be. And your head all but explodes with conflicting thoughts. They try to take over. The bastards. They can crush your spirit and soul, if you let them. Each willing to give whatever it takes for dominance. A nasty fight to the death.

I *thought* I was managing it all just fine, until a colleague, and good friend, approached me in my classroom early one morning several months back, and handed me a business card. It was for a therapist.

"Call her. She's good people," he said in his slow bass playing hippy voice. He turned and left.

And I did eventually call her. I arrived at my first

appointment in grand style. I was running late and zipping around the back streets trying to find her address. I zoomed past it, stopped suddenly, made an abrupt U-turn, and wheeled up to the front of her house. But I never saw the deep street gutter and my front wheel jammed in hard. I felt my passenger front end sink.

"Shit!" I screamed. I got out, walked around to the front of my car, and out of frustration, kicked the hell out of my wheel.

"Diane?" I heard. It was the sweetest of voices.

There she was. My new therapist. Standing on her front porch, smiling and waving.

I walked up to her, introduced myself, and said, "I'm going to need a tow truck."

Classic first impression, I thought. We stood on her front porch looking out at my car. And she paused long enough for me to see it. To *feel* it. I was my car. Smashed and barely functional. And desperately needing a lift.

"You have your work cut out for you," I told her early on. "I've been stifling shit down for years."

And I had been. Deep down. But the divorce lifted the cap and all those emotions exploded out like a shaken bottle of soda. It was unpredictable and messy. We worked through it though. Slowly. Each appointment I rambled on and on about the weather and my job, waiting for the last ten minutes to vomit it all up.

"I'll see you in two days," she said smiling.

"Don't most people do this once a week?" I asked.

"You're not most people," she said in her most gentle voice.

Therapy was exhausting. But necessary. It's where I first

learned about the generations of family patterns. Breaking the cycle. Trusting your intuition. Finding your center. I learned about love and light and letting go. I learned that I was worth the work. And that healing was possible.

Divorce and therapy left me searching for clarity, fighting my way back from the edge, wanting to reconnect with some kind of feeling, and desperately seeking forgiveness. But forgiveness for what? For being gay? For being honest and brave enough to live my truth? Or for walking away from a vow that I made? Was I running *from* something? Or *to* something? I simply had no idea. But I knew in that moment I was willing to try anything to feel whole again. And I seemingly put myself in a situation where I was going to have nothing but time to figure it all out.

*

My African hut came with a wheelbarrow, two host families, and a set of rules I couldn't quite wrap my head around. The wheelbarrow was to carry water up from the stream. It was a vibrant stream, and the local water source for the nearby village. It was the gathering place for African women. A place to do laundry. Sing. And gossip about the White American girl on top of the hill.

The stream sat just below my outhouse. The hill to and from was daunting, but manageable. Less so in the rain. I remember thinking they were awfully close — my outhouse and the stream. I imagined it was a direct route, from my ass to the hole to the stream. I inquired about it. My concerns were quickly dismissed. It was brought up that I was a woman and, as a result, not knowledgeable of those things. And also, that I was not a civil engineer. For sure I am not a civil engineer. But still, they seemed awfully close.

*

My two host families couldn't have been more different. One family lived just next door to my hut. They were modern, and very nice, gentle, and welcoming people. The other, far more traditional, family, lived down the hill and toward the center of the village. They were abrasive and unpredictable. Within hours of my arrival, the modern host-father marched me down the hill to meet my very traditional host-father. The three of us stood in the doorway of his small concrete house like an African re-make of *My Two Dads*.

There, I was introduced to my co-host father, the Tribal Chief of the village, and principal of the school I was assigned to. Tribal Chief? What are the protocols with this? I wondered.

I held my hand out to shake his hand, which was not at all the protocol. A woman should not shake a man's hand, particularly if he is a chief. I tried to recover by making a small joke about Chief Wahoo, the former logo of the Cleveland Indians. No one laughed. I tried to explain further, "You know baseball? I grew up with Chief Wahoo. He's the logo for the team. Not to be confused with Slider, of course. He's the real mascot. Two very different things," I said.

I suddenly realized I was yelling. Screaming at a tribal chief about one of the most offensive American baseball logos. Like the louder I yelled, the more he would understand what I was saying.

The following morning, I was mulling around my hut trying to tie my skirt, or sarong, when I heard from behind my door a soft, "Ko Ko."

I kept fiddling with my skirt and looking at the stack of dishes in my bucket. Quite a few given the short time I've been here, I thought.

"Ko Ko!" I heard again.

Then, I remembered. Physical knocking on a door is not customary. The Basotho people just stand outside of the door and say two short words. Ko Ko. Interesting concept, really. It's a custom I'd like to see adopted in America, actually. It's so much softer, the verbal greeting. As if to say, "Hey friend, I'm just here spreading love and joy." Knocking is so aggressive. And the doorbell is like a hammer to the head.

"Ko Ko!" The echo ricochet off my one continuous round wall.

I opened the door and the Tribal Chief shouted, "They should have taught you that in training! Come! We foot it now," he said escorting me off to my first day of school.

Ok, maybe not so peaceful after all. And we did foot it. For several miles. Uphill. Seemingly both ways.

*

To the surprise of no one, I had the hardest time adjusting to the rules. *Skirts always.* Not only did my fellow volunteers lend me skirts, they also taught me how to wear them. A skill, of which, I never quite mastered.

Don't leave your hut after dark. Hence, the pee bucket. Point noted.

Always greet the locals. And by this, it means you are expected to stop and have comprehensive conversations with anyone greeting you and/or asking you questions. 'Where are you coming from' really means, stop and tell me your life story. And conversely, 'Where are you going' means stop here with me for an hour and tell me all of your hopes and dreams for the future. Simply saying, "I'm going to the post office," is not entirely rude, but it is not at all sufficient. They want to know why you are going to the post office, who are you posting a letter to, and for how long you will be there. And, might you stop anywhere else on your journey?

But the absolute hardest rule for me to follow? *Women do not drink alcohol in public. Or swear.* Undoubtedly, two of my favorite pastimes.

Also, being gay in a very conservative country run by kings and chiefs is a tricky situation, for sure. Don't be fooled by two men walking down a dirt road in a Lesotho village holding hands. They are likely not gay at all. It is a sign of friendship. Camaraderie. Our bravado American culture can be skittish about such a display of public affection. In American culture, men are mostly raised to bond over guns and beer.

It's actually good they taught us about the hand holding in Africa School, because otherwise I would have thought I hit the jackpot of placements. I recently came out gay and they placed me in the only gay village in Africa? Whoa! What are the odds?

A gazillion to one. Those are the odds.

So, at a time when I was just coming out, and really exploring my truth, I had to quietly go back into the closet.

Not only that, but upon first glance, I was also the only White person around. Upon second and third glances, and even a fourth really hard, deep look for miles and miles, I was still the only White person around. Being the only White person, and especially female, in a small, rural, African village is a lot like living in a fishbowl. With no other fish. Or even a small piece of greenery to distract the attention of onlookers. I became an attention magnet and instant celebrity. I couldn't take a shit without the villagers knowing.

Literally, my outhouse was on top of a hill in clear view of the village below. Anyone with moderately good eyesight could see me march from my hut to the outhouse. I could almost hear them mumbling, "The American is shitting, *again.*"

The outhouse became so much more to me than just a bathroom. It was my saving grace. My escape from reality. My own glorious tin throne. I permanently installed reading material on the walls to enjoy while I sat there, contemplating my life's choices. Comic strips, newspaper articles, and pictures were taped all over, just in case I was overcome by a sense of urgency and didn't have time to grab some proper reading material. It was my way of executing toilet preparedness, and some level of control over my affairs.

There are three assumptions when you are an American *in* Africa: 1. You are rich. 2. Everything you do is fascinating. 3. You carry a pound of candy or "sweets" with you everywhere you go.

Early on in my stay, I decided to take a jog through the village. Within minutes, I had a handful of small children following me. "Sweets?" they shouted. After about ten minutes, there were probably twice as many kids. It got so intense at one point, I wasn't sure if I was being chased or if they were joining in the exercise. When I finally reached my destination, I thought, this must be how Rocky felt running through Philadelphia and up the steps to the Art Museum.

The days rolled on slowly. I got as busy as one could get in the situation. I footed it up to my school every day. Some days, I arrived to empty classrooms.

"Ah, they are off to get firewood for lunch," the Tribal Chief would say.

Other days, I arrived to classrooms packed full of eager students with no teachers. "Ah, 'tis payday. They are all at the bank," he would say.

I was always so amazed at how a room full of students could sit so quietly without any adult supervision whatsoever. They would quietly wait for their teacher to show; sometimes for hours, before slowly dispersing to return home, not having any food or lessons that day.

Most days, though, I jumped in to teach lessons on grammar. Or vocabulary. They enjoyed grammar far more than any group of students I had ever worked with. Then again, I was Rocky Balboa status.

I figured out how to acquire lukewarm beer. And I drank it with the bo-'me, or Basotho women, in accordance with the local norms. In private, out of a paper bag, and wearing skirts. Confirming my philosophy that there's no better way to immerse yourself in a culture like drinking with the natives. I learned all kinds of stuff. Tricks of the trade. Including how to carry the bucket of water *on* your head. "You just walk. Don't drop it," they shared.

I never thought of that, I told them. And we all connected through the universal language of laughter.

I read so many books that I started re-reading them just to pass the time. I read *The Poisonwood Bible* three times. And obsessively trekked to the post office in search of mail.

My dad regularly sent newspaper clippings of basketball

games and political cartoons, which inevitably made it to my outhouse wall. He included the recent obituaries, "just for fun," he wrote. The clippings were accompanied by letters I could barely read because his handwriting was so terrible. "Well, you up and left us," he wrote one time. And, "We almost have a president," he wrote a few lines later. They were the only legible lines of the whole letter.

My mom took to writing poetry, which was sweet, but also weird. She rambled on and on that I was the sunshine of her eyes and how me leaving for Africa left a giant, gaping hole in her heart. Uplifting stuff, really. Her letters were neatly typed, double spaced, and incredibly well-written. Signed at the bottom, "Mom."

And nothing made me feel more special like getting a "Family Memo" from my brother. Spaced perfectly on his company letterhead, in Memorandum style. He mustered up a good 8–10 sentences about the current state of affairs, a few notes about my checking account, and how much he hated Ohio weather. Included in those lines, some hint that he read my last letter to him, though usually a bit off on the details. He typed out his full name, followed by his credentials. In blue ink just to the left, his handwritten initials. It was a nice gesture, of course, but it left me feeling like one of his clients.

My sister also sent me letters. It was clear who she got her penmanship from, because they looked a lot like my fathers. She also included a newspaper clipping or two about the Amish, a new local barn-raising, and some notes about her latest adventure at the Flea Market. It looked like she was on a roller coaster when she wrote it, and I couldn't quite tell if she bought the baskets from the Amish or if she thought the Amish was a racket.

She also gave me some family scoop. "Dad spent the weekend on suicide watch," she wrote. And there were a few lines about a knife and 9–1–1, but I couldn't quite make out *who* was doing what. Then finally, "so his relationships are going well." A little down the page, a story about her husband coaching my niece's T-ball team. Cute, I thought. Then, "But he calls them all little fuckers so I don't think it's going to work out."

*

My family showed regard for me in unusual ways. While in Africa, I saw them each through a different lens. Outside of family holidays. Through letters they pieced together. A real effort to reach out. Connect from afar. I come from a fairly cold family with a dark sense of humor. Generations of such qualities, actually. You'll never hear "I love you." But you'll get a clip upside the head, some sarcastic banter, and a "Get your ass over here and have a beer with me." A real supernova of affection. I was thousands of miles away from home, and got family memos, obituaries, letters with a few funny lines, full names spelled out like court documents, and handwritten initials. Absent were any real terms of endearment. No 'I love you's.' Or, 'We're so proud of you.' But I knew they did. And they were. And I missed them all in some weird way.

*

When I wasn't scouring for mail, I would foot it across the village to connect with my friend, and former roommate from Africa School. I was surprised by her American-like set up.

213

She stayed in a real structure, with electricity. She could take hot showers. Make phone calls. And watch television with her host family. She clearly gave a better description of how she wanted to spend her two years. I saw her living quarters and instantly regretted telling them I wanted to be dropped off by a helicopter in the middle of nowhere.

We would hitch a ride to the next village to hang out with other volunteers. For longer treks, we'd wait all day at the taxi rink for a minivan to fill with enough people to depart. We stretched out on a rock under the hot sun. Read. Talked. It was another good opportunity to contemplate all your life's choices. You can really get to know a person when you're waiting all day in a taxi rink with them. And then finally, just before sunset, the driver would announce, "We try again tomorrow." And we would do it all over again the next day.

When we did get together, we were giddy with excitement. We'd swap books, exchange Africa stories, and freely talk in English. It was refreshing to have someone fully understand the words that were coming out of my mouth. We pieced together meals, drank warm beer, and hung out in our pajamas. Sometimes we got high on Matekoane, or weed, and laughed ourselves to sleep.

I absolutely loved hanging out with Peace Corps hippies. Their genuine kindness and generosity filled my heart and soul. During one get together, I arrived late in the evening and was instantly handed a piece of food. "Here, this one didn't have as many flies on it."

Back home, that food would have been thrown away. Discarded entirely. But here, in a small hut in the middle of Africa, it is delicious. And the act of selecting a piece of food based on how few flies were on it says, "Hey, you are special and we appreciate you." Also, it says, "Please don't shit your brains out in my hut tonight." But getting together with them scratched my homesick itch, for at least a little while.

*

At some point, I became so sick that I had explosive diarrhea and vomited non-stop for days. I was completely over the outhouse situation. I managed to hitch a ride back to the capital city and Peace Corps house. I barely survived the six-hour drive of windy roads and sketchy cliffs. Guardrails hadn't quite made it to the mountain roads of Lesotho and so essentially, every twist and turn could easily be your last. In fact, I made it a habit not to look down as we rounded a treacherous turn because inevitably you would see smashed up white taxi vans crushed to death after careening off the mountainside. Unable to be fixed, they lay, untouched, slowly rotting away, one day at a time. Kind of like my intestines.

*

I couldn't sit upright without cramping and having the urge to vomit. So, I lay, cockeyed, trying hard to focus on something solid on the front dashboard. I would have laid down entirely except that I had to share the back seat with a handful of chickens. The smell was awful, and those fuckers never shut up. Moving around. Pecking their heads off. Screeching whenever the hell they felt like it. One of them took to my lap and I fully expected to find a few eggs in my crotch upon our arrival.

The other thing about the wonderful Basotho people is

that they love their music. They love it so much that they want everyone in the surrounding five square miles to also share in the joy. So, they blast it at an intolerable decibel. And it's not like it's a peaceful type of music, or even Caribbean-like. That's a music you can easily tolerate if it was blaring. Because it has some rhythm. And it makes sense. It sounds like music. When you hear Caribbean music, it transports you to a happy place, where you feel like you are sitting poolside holding a cocktail with an umbrella in it.

Sotho music is a lot like loud, angry screaming. I'm sure it's rich in many cultural aspects using a variety of native instruments, but not understanding the language or really able to fully appreciate it, to me it just sounded a lot like someone is five seconds from being murdered. It's the kind of music that could be used to torture someone into spilling super-spy secrets. If you put a person in a small room, or car with the windows rolled up, and just exposed them to Sotho music at that volume, for hours, anyone would crack. Wars would end abruptly. "Nice job, Sherman," you would hear. "That music gets 'em every time," they would say packing all their shit up to go home.

I finally arrived to the Peace Corps house, and had never been so happy to be sitting completely still, in the quiet. Though, the music continued to ring in my ears for a little while longer. Every now and then, I would shake my head trying to get rid of the sounds. Sotho music is the gift that keeps on giving, I thought.

I was incredibly sick and feeling scared, so I called my mom. She wasn't my usual go to in these kinds of situations as she hasn't historically given the best advice. I was in no mood to hear about astrological orbits and how I haven't had a

Jupiter rising in quite some time. But I was desperate, and sometimes you just want your mom. So, I called her.

She, of course, felt helpless. Being so far away there wasn't much she could do. "Go to the hospital," she pleaded.

I told her I would look into it, hung up, and then passed out.

I woke up in a strange room. Sweating. Empty Gatorade packets surrounded me. A fellow Peace Corps volunteer walked in to check on me.

"Oh, you're awake," I heard. "The doctor was here. Gave you Gatorade to hydrate. Gotta' love Africa," she said laughing.

"How long was I out?" I asked.

"A while," she said. "Your mom has been calling," she added.

*

Without any formal medical intervention, unless you count a gallon of Gatorade as a 'therapeutic dose', I eventually returned to my hut in the rural village. But I couldn't quite get over feeling sick. All the time. At the thought of food. Certain smells. Sudden movements. It was a terrible feeling.

After a few weeks I wasn't feeling any better, so I made the trek into town to call the Peace Corps doctor. "Send me a stool sample," she said.

"How does *that* work?" I asked.

A few days later a man in a white Peace Corps Safari Land Rover showed up at my hut door to collect my little jar of poop.

"Do you have a seatbelt for this?" I asked handing it to him.

He did not laugh. And he promptly drove off.

*

As much as I wanted to tough it out through my full two-year commitment, I was reaching my limit. But I was determined to make the trek to nearby Cape Town, South Africa. Thanks to my first teaching job, I immersed myself in South African history. I admired Nelson Mandela and his long walk to freedom. He spent twenty-seven years in prison for fighting against Apartheid, ultimately rising up to become the first Black head of state and democratically elected president. A remarkable legacy. And I wanted to see as much of it as I could before leaving the continent. As such, I arranged to take a holiday and meet up with a fellow volunteer over the upcoming Easter weekend.

At the time I was a Peace Corps volunteer in 2001, the crime rate was off the chart. In 2001, a South African was more likely to be murdered than die in a car crash. And there were a lot of car crashes. Also, at that time, the rate of HIV/AIDS infections spiked exponentially, and it was the leading cause of death in Africa. There were about 28 million people living with HIV/AIDS throughout Sub-Sahara Africa. Of those 28 million people, 55% were women. To round all of that out, the average life expectancy in South Africa in 2001 was 47 years old, a far cry from 66 if AIDS had *not* been a factor.

I say all of that to say, it was a terrible time to be lollygagging around South Africa. In my rural village, I felt protected and looked after. Outside of that bubble, in the streets of Cape Town, I was going to be on my own. Being a Peace Corps volunteer did afford you a little advantage, for sure. Thanks to Africa School, we were equipped with language skills and survival techniques. But ultimately, I was going to have to earn my street cred.

Immediately upon arrival, I was confronted with the country's looming taxi wars. Around the fall of Apartheid in 1994, commuters were often the target of violence as political unrest spilled out into all parts of life. The transportation industry was largely unregulated, and as competition became fierce, taxi operators used mafia-like techniques to win business. As soon as I arrived, it became instantly clear that, while Apartheid was over, blatant racism was still very much a thing.

From everything I had read, Black taxis, or minibuses, were readily available. And cheap. The 16-seat Toyota Quantum buses, which still prevail today, transported South Africans to and from the Townships, or *shanty towns*. The vehicles were not always roadworthy, and the drivers were notorious for disregarding safety measures and the general rules of the road. They were often way over-crowded, dangerous, and the only public transit that would travel into unsafe areas, like the Townships. The experience in a Black taxi was unpredictable. Hence, cheap transportation.

White Taxis, on the other hand, were private cars driven by white drivers. They were far more expensive. They were regulated and safe, of course. Though they did have some travel restrictions. They would not travel into certain areas perceived as unsafe; or otherwise, socially unacceptable for a white person to visit.

As I stood on the side of the road, desperately needing a ride, I was accosted by a white guy holding open the door of a small, private car. It reminded me of the first time I saw a white guy in South Africa months earlier. For whatever reason, I expected him to speak English. Naive, I know. He did not. He was an Afrikaner, and spoke Afrikaans. Which is not at all like English. Anyway, I asked how much for the ride and was appalled at the cost. Having been a Peace Corps volunteer all of five months, I became accustomed to a certain kind of lifestyle. Hitchhiking. Sleeping in precarious situations. Poor toilet accommodations. And riding in very unsafe, overly crowded minivans. Usually with a variety of livestock.

I didn't trust the guy. My gut said no.

I glanced across the street and saw a Black Taxi, just about filled to the brim. Curious faces stared out the windows. The driver hollered something to me, and I asked how much. It was far more reasonable. People on the bus started waving me over. So, I made my way across the street and the white taxi driver started waving his arms and shouting in broken English, "That's a Black taxi, not for white people!" He was pissed. He kept pointing to his car, like it was a gift from God. And as I crossed the street, ignoring his remarks, the entire bus erupted in shouting and laughter. By the time I stepped onto the bus, they were all clapping and singing. One lady quickly moved over to make room for me. They were so happy I got on that bus. Or, more likely, happy that the white guy lost a fare. And then the driver blared Sotho music. It pierced my ears. And I instantly felt nauseous. Of course, Sotho music. What else would it be?

Prior to the trip, I had studied Townships, which were underdeveloped racially segregated urban areas, or settlements, that lay just outside of a more developed city. Otherwise known as a *shanty town*, or *slum,* they were filled with improvised structures, or shacks, made of mud and wood. Townships often lacked basic infrastructure. Without electricity or a formal water and sewage system, residents were more susceptible to disease. And violence. Townships struggled with overcrowded schools, a high dropout rate, and a lack of fundamental resources like clean water and food. As a result, gangs, crime, and death were prevalent.

Townships were segregated by color: Black, Colored's, and non-Whites. Non-White Townships were reserved for Asian/Indians, a group that saw a growth of almost 6.5% in just five years. Though separated by color, they all shared one common trait — poverty. Most women were employed as domestic workers and took the long taxi rides into Cape Town. The men who could find work, often set out for the mines, an inherently dangerous job that forced them to be away from their families for months at a time. The residents of these Townships played an integral role in South African history and the anti-Apartheid movement. They were a proud people who suffered greatly. A hidden force. And I felt compelled to see them all first-hand.

I connected with my fellow Peace Corps volunteer, and we did what every good tourist on vacation does. We hired a couple of bodyguards. I'm adventurous, not stupid.

Early the next morning, two Black South African guys showed up to our hostel, wearing white Oxford button-down long-sleeve shirts and dark pants. They both wore dark sunglasses and carried black jackets, folded neatly over their arms.

Holy shit, I thought.

When they weren't looking, we whispered to each other like a couple of smitten schoolgirls.

"They look legit," she said.

"Right?" I responded.

"Do you think they have guns?" she asked.

"I hope so," I replied. "You can't just walk around looking like that and *not* have a gun," I surmised.

And off we went. Over the next few days, I saw more than I ever imagined. I walked the streets of various Townships. The smell was almost too much to bear. Burning garbage. Dead animals. Overflowing outhouses. We met local residents. They were a proud people. And generous. We were invited in for food, of which I could not eat because my intestines rumbled continuously. We toured Soweto and I saw Nelson Mandela's birthplace. We took the ferry to Robben Island and I stood in his prison cell. I tried to make sense of it all. He served more time in prison than I had been alive. He fought tirelessly for the disenfranchised. For equal rights and justice. For *human rights*. In that moment, I felt compelled to make good use of my time on Earth.

*

My leave eventually ended, and I made the trek back to my village. From the taxi rink, I walked by the post office to collect my mail. I opened the one letter I had been waiting for. It was from the Peace Corps doctor and contained the results of my stool sample.

Handwritten and barely legible, two simple sentences. "Your stool sample is clear. I hope you feel better."

*

I stayed a few more weeks, only to turn around and head back to Cape Town. This time, I met up with another volunteer for an entirely different kind of experience. We ventured out to wine country, and sipped Pinotage and enjoyed beautiful mountain views. We went to a gay club. We even played with penguins on the Cape. We enjoyed each other and all that an authentic African experience brings. Our time ended and she returned to her village. But I stayed a bit longer.

I wandered around Cape Town in my own way. Exploring a different scene entirely. Meeting people who were on real adventures. A couple of Australian guys embarking on a motorcycle trip to northern Africa. A lone girl traveling around, taking pictures, and writing a book. One evening, completely stoned, I piled into a VW bus and headed to Camps Bay to enjoy the sunset on the beach with complete strangers.

*

I didn't want to leave. I imagined living there forever. I envisioned a life of adventure and meaningful work. But I was growing weary of the hut and chaotic job situation. And feeling sick all the time. It wasn't entirely working for me. I called my brother to see how much money I had in the bank. I told him my plan to stay or venture off to Europe for a while. "You don't have that kind of money," he said laughing. "Just come home."

Do I return to life as I know it? Plop right back down into a life of familiarity and the status quo? I was forever changed by this experience. I was an entirely new person from when I last stepped foot on American soil. I was at a crossroads.

*

Ultimately, the Peace Corps called me AWOL. I called it exploring my options. They tracked me down and implored me to return immediately. They needed a decision from me regarding my future commitment with the Peace Corps. I had to make a decision. Within just a few hours of my return to Maseru, Lesotho, I was bustled into a Peace Corps Safari Land Rover and driven back to my hut. I had the night to pack and say my goodbyes to my host family. It's funny, it took me months to pack for Africa, and only a few hours to pack to go home.

*

I was sitting on the dirt floor of my hut. Amidst the same buckets, though far more weathered. As was I. And fifteen pounds lighter. It didn't take long to pack what little I had decided to take home. Letters I received. My backpack. An African wool blanket. A drum I bought off a street vendor in the city. And my guitar that I never learned to play.

*

Word quickly got out that I was leaving my village because I had a "Ko Ko" at my door late into the night. I would never have opened the door so late except it was a woman and one of the Peace Corps workers was staying in the hut next door. So, I opened the door. She was wearing a colorful scarf, wrapped tightly around her head and down over the right side of her face.

"Oh, why not. Come on in," I said.

224

I offered her a seat and she proceeded to tell me a long, complicated story in Sesotho that I couldn't quite follow. Something about a dog and money. The only two words I recognized. I sat staring at her intensely, trying to remember all of my Sesotho words but nothing rang a bell.

Suddenly, she unwrapped her scarf to unveil a missing ear and deep scar down to the lower part of her right cheek.

"Jesus!" I said. It was a terrible sight. I was feeling fortunate in that moment, though, that she wasn't actually holding the ear in her hand, as if to say, a dog bit my ear off, can you please re-attach this?

"Oh, I see," I said cringing. "You can wrap it back up," I said motioning the act of wrapping a scarf around my head.

It became apparent that she wanted money for a surgery. And I had to communicate that I didn't, in fact, have that kind of money for her, as sad as her situation was and all. Not an easy string of words to put together in another language. My heart broke for her, and I did my best to communicate that. Nevertheless, I escorted her to the door and thanked her for coming.

*

Early the following morning, I was driven back to the Peace Corps house and given one night to say goodbye to my fellow volunteers. There were a few who made the long trek back to see me off. It was nice to re-connect with friends. The same people I left America with. We grew close with this shared experience. It's funny how a group of people can share the same experience but have very different outcomes. Leave with varying degrees of happiness and perspectives of individual accomplishments or successes.

Upon arrival, we played the 'who is going to leave first' game. Admittedly, I thought I would outlast many. Not all, but many. One young man, so eager to have landed in Africa, sketched everything he saw. We'd be out walking, and he would just take a knee, and sketch something. His enthusiasm boiled over. "That can't last long," I said jokingly. "He's going to wear out before we finish training," I added. And he did. A few others, who I was certain would not last, stood in front of me on my last night in Africa, telling *me* goodbye. "Have a McDonalds cheeseburger for us," they said.

It was a conflicting time filled with a mix of emotions, for sure. I wasn't entirely sure I made the right decision to leave early, but once I uttered the words, momentum took over and it became another journey entirely.

*

The thing about Africa is that it heightens your senses and evokes emotion in ways you never imagined. Whatever you might feel in normal situations is magnified exponentially. Prior to Africa, I enjoyed a nice sunset. In Africa, sunsets creeped out of the sky and seeped slowly into my soul. The same is true for bug bites. Or intestinal distress. At home, they are inconvenient. In Africa, they are pus-filled pockets of infection or gut-wrenching diarrhea.

Individual senses heighten to new levels; but collectively, they can flood your brain. And with prolonged exposure to such intense experiences, one can easily fall victim to sensory overload. An inability to make sound decisions based on an objective thought. Emotional fatigue, even.

To my surprise, while in Africa, I found love. Love for a country. Love for a people. Love for a purpose in life outside of myself. Love for a beautiful soul. Love for myself, even. I found myself giving and receiving it in ways I had never experienced. Or ever thought possible. The exchange of such things intersecting in a way that tears the walls down, breaks through barriers, opens your heart enough to invite others in; and conversely, let go of others who no longer belong.

My time in Africa also taught me that time is relative and to expect the unexpected. I learned that your survival depends on your ability to adapt, and your willingness to persevere through uncomfortable times. Waiting in a taxi rink all day is frustrating, but you find some joy in hanging out with a friend. Finding out there aren't enough people to fill a taxi so you have to try it again the next day, can take you to a whole other level.

Hearing a native say, "I'm coming," is not at all a sexual reference. It simply means they are going to visit you at some point in the future. It could be later that day. Tomorrow. Or in three months. One never really knows in Africa. And, in the end, it doesn't really matter because you aren't all that busy. You have the time to wait.

*

Watching a dog run around a field, free of a leash and collar, makes you smile and lean into the moment. It reminds you of your childhood pet. Playing and training it with enthusiasm. Witnessing a lone Basotho man walk by and shoot the dog dead forces you to understand the brutality of a country where dogs who run wild are not pets. They are dangerous and unpredictable.

The starkness of those moments is enough to make you pause and think, What the fuck? But those are the moments that define the African experience. A truly authentic experience.

Admittedly, I was not the quintessential Peace Corps volunteer. I didn't fully prepare. I became distracted with my own stuff. And I left before fully realizing my potential as a volunteer. But I understood the spirit of it all, and inevitably learned the Peace Corps way. For a short time, I did become a part of something much larger than myself. Contributed in a way that was meaningful. But I never got to a point where it was sustainable. There's no quantifiable way to know if Lesotho was a better place because of me. But undoubtedly, I was in a better place because of Lesotho.

And just like that, I was on a plane to America. But I wasn't just going back to America. I was going back to all the things I ran away from months earlier. My family, a budding relationship with a woman, and a teaching career. Those things were the same, but I was different. Substantially so. I had no idea how to marry the two, but I knew that I had just turned the corner on finding peace.

Part IIII
A Twilight Zone

19

A Tale of Two Ships

At 78 and 80, my parents haven't changed much. They have weathered the storm a lot like a couple of old wooden ships. Deep cracks run along the surface, loud creaks emerge with every twist and turn, and their engines have been cleaned out, updated, and restored as much as possible given their age and lifestyles. They still move, but at a much slower pace. And they don't venture too far from shore. They often forget where they're heading or where they just came from. And they struggle to keep up with the sudden changes in wind direction. But fundamentally, at their core, they authentically maintain the spirit of old wooden ships. Steadfast in their ways. Unique in character. And oblivious to those around them.

My parents have run parallel courses. Separate, but always within sight of each other. They have been divorced for over forty-five years but have never lived more than a few miles apart. My mom studies astrology and repeatedly tells me that my father's moon sits directly on her sun. Which to me, sounds a lot like he's been a major pain in her ass for years. But the synastry of their sun/moon connection is real. It has endured through the years and has kept them on the same chartered course.

My mom will tell you that my dad changed after having kids. A switch flipped. He couldn't take the responsibility. That he became volatile.

My dad will tell you that she was too sensitive and didn't stand up for herself. "If she just told me to shut up, well then I would have just shut up," he said to me many years later over beers. "I didn't have anywhere else to go. I would have fallen in line eventually," he mused.

Both are right. Except he never would have fallen in line and she had every right to make the decision she made, under the circumstances.

Over the years my parents have attended their grandchildren's games, graduation parties, and a myriad of other events that required them to sit near each other and talk. They never *looked* divorced. In the almost fifty years I've been alive, I don't recall one boisterous argument between the two of them. I was fortunate enough to have escaped the tragic court hearings, custody battles, and nasty fights. It just wasn't like that. *They* weren't like that.

It's not to say they don't have their differences. Because they do. Or that either of them ever wanted to jump right back into the thing. Because they haven't. There's simply a fondness there. A sun/moon synastry. But underneath it all, there's a firm "You stay in your port, and I'll stay in mine."

With torn sails and shabby navigational skills, they're now sailing through their twilight years like a couple of drunken sailors. They say whatever they want, show complete disregard for their own health, or the impact of such things on others, and move through the days with reckless abandon. Which makes sense, if you think about it, because it's exactly how we were raised.

Somehow, my siblings and I managed to raise ourselves, and now, collectively, are attempting to parent our own parents. And they, in turn, are being parented in a way that they, themselves, never subscribed to.

There's been no mention of regret or shame in any way. No apologies. Just a 'we did the best we could at the time" kind of thing. And, "You all turned out just fine."

For years, my siblings and I have been just plugging along, muddling through the days, trying to live our best lives. Since returning from the Peace Corps, I went to grad school to become a school psychologist and am now working primarily with students with emotional challenges. It's funny how the universe works. I essentially became the thing I needed the most when I was a kid in school. And I got married again, which is a thing I never thought possible for me. She is wonderful, puts up with my antics, and, as it turns out, is the final piece to my very complex puzzle.

My brother channeled his electrical skills to become an engineer, which he quickly grew tired of, and is now selling commercial real estate in south Florida. He is known in his world as the closer because he has turned closing difficult deals into an art form. Not too bad for a long-haired drummer boy who almost set the house on fire and got his high school diploma in the mail.

And my sister has spent years working with young children with disabilities and elderly clients in a nursing home. She quickly became known for taking on all the tough cases, like complicated health issues or wildly eccentric behaviors. No matter what her elderly clients called her, she always dressed them up, put lipstick on them, and positioned them in a chair, like royalty, in preparation for a family visit.

It's a common theme for all three of us, complicated cases. We seem to gravitate toward the thing nobody else wants.

But now, the three of us are on a new kind of journey, not entirely unlike the uncharted territory of our childhood, where we were dodging obstacles, barely avoiding disaster, and figuring it all out as we went.

My brother and I both live out of state; thereby, leaving my sister, who remains in our hometown, to manage much of the day-to-day parental challenges. She undoubtedly bears a great deal of the burden, for which my brother and I are forever grateful. Much like a ship taking on water, she is constantly in motion bailing it out, with a tiny bucket.

Caring for aging parents can strain a sibling relationship. Someone does too much. Another not enough. A third needs constantly brought into the loop. Resentments can build if you let them. As a crew, we have moved into action trying to save these sinking ships. Tempers fly. Fears heighten. Uncertainty lingers. Our sense of humor is the last life raft and all that we have left to survive this experience.

I recently brought my mother back to stay with my wife and I, for a short visit, to give my sister a break. My brother called and left me a voice message saying it was a terrible time to have my mom visit because the COVID-19 pandemic makes evicting tenants virtually impossible. "You'll never get her out of your house as long as this pandemic is here," he said laughing.

And my sister, when I was trying to understand my mom's complicated medication regiment and asked how she had been keeping up with it all. "I haven't killed her yet," she said.

We now find ourselves in the late stage of the game, faced with increasingly more complex situations like navigating terminal illnesses, daunting medical appointments, and fading memories. All while trying to expand our empathetic capacity for our parents and such things. Honestly, we're all just trying to stay afloat as much as possible. But they're not making it easy for us.

For the past forty years, my father has eaten diner food, and bar hopped his way through the day. The only healthy thing in his refrigerator is water. It's also the *only* thing in his refrigerator. Tall, strong, and lean for most of his life, he now looks a lot like a squatter who has settled into an abandoned house and refuses to leave.

Upon moving into the house he currently lives in, my father immediately erected tarps in the doorways to keep the heat in, placed a toilet in the middle of the kitchen, for convenience, and stationed a large plastic jug of water on the counter next to the kitchen sink. He fills it with water recycled from the dehumidifier in the basement. The water jug has a metal faucet attached to the thing. It's a brilliant contraption, by the way, because it's a convenient way to have running water without actually *paying* for running water.

His entire house is unsafe and in complete disarray. There are large holes in the floor, and with one wrong step, you might suddenly find yourself in the basement, which is a terrible place to be. With each visit I make, there is some new outrageous contraption that he designed as a matter of convenience, or simply, as a product of his own imagination.

Rather than pay for cable, he dragged a roof-sized antenna into his living room and attached it to his small black and white television. To eliminate the need for leaning forward to switch his three channels, he invented a 'grabber', a long wooden pole with a mechanism on the end to do the work for him.

Also, anything less than five pounds in his living space is duck taped to a large red brick. I asked him about this one time, when I picked up the phone to use it and noticed it was duck taped to a brick.

"I like things to have some weight to them," he said matter of factly.

Strewn about the room are a handful of telephone books rolled up tightly and duck taped. A few have a towel wrapped around them, also duck taped. Seeing them placed on each end of his couch like bookends suggests they are pillows. That makes sense, I thought.

When I saw the same telephone book contraption in his car I was confused.

"Dad, what is the rolled-up phone book for?" I asked.

"Well, if you think I'm going to tell you all my secrets, you have another thing coming," he said. "But if you guess it correctly, I'll tell you if you're right," he finished.

This led to a week-long Facebook discussion about all the potential uses of a rolled-up telephone book, of which, he said, were not correct.

*

To round out my father's squatter decor, a loaded shotgun is always leaning up against the wall, just next to his broken recliner. He doesn't even try to hide the bullets, which lay next to the phone duck taped to a brick.

About a year ago, my mom stepped foot into his house, only by default because she was riding with me and I needed to drop something off for him. She got about five steps in, saw his living conditions and screamed, "What the hell is wrong with you? Your parents didn't raise you like this!"

And she stormed out.

*

I called my dad not long ago because I heard he was up on a ladder doing something on his roof. I thought it seemed dangerous for an 80-year-old guy. I told him as such.

"Well obviously you have me mistaken for somebody who gives a shit," he said.

I suspect I had that coming, what with expressing my concern for his safety and all.

He quickly followed it up with, "How else are things going to get done around here?"

Fair question, I thought.

"Are *you* going to come over to do it?" he asked with biting sarcasm.

"Well don't be silly, dad. No, no, I'm not," I answered. Followed by, "We've established I'm not good with manual labor, so climb away."

My mom, on the other hand, resides in a very tight-knit retirement community. She is a thirty-year diabetic who reaps all the side-effects of that. Extreme highs and lows with sugar, on and off confusion, and neuropathy. She also has increasingly poor balance and mobility. For my mother, diabetes, next to being born the day after Christmas, is the bane of her existence.

"I just took the day off, Diane, sue me," she barked one day after waking up on the floor in front of her refrigerator with a jar of peanut butter in her lap.

"Mom, diabetes isn't just a thing you can take a break from," I replied.

"Well, I'm calling in sick for a few days," she proclaimed.

"Mom, what does that even mean?" I asked.

And getting her to her medical appointments can be a full-time job. She doesn't drive, and one time it took my sister and I five phone calls to arrange for her ride to the doctor. Later that afternoon I called to ask about the appointment and heard, "Oh dear, she canceled her appointment earlier in the day."

*

After a fair amount of discussion about my mom's financial situation, my siblings and I collaborated on a plan to manage her spending. I signed her up for online banking, created a password, and began sifting through it all. Turns out, she had racked up all kind of credit card debt and was nickel and diming money away to her neighbors. Five dollars here. Fifteen dollars there.

"Mom, why are you giving money to your neighbors?" I asked her after going through her account.

"Well, they asked to borrow money," she said matter of factly.

"Are they paying you back?" I asked.

Long pause.

"I think so," she finally said.

The thing about my mom is she can't remember things like she used to. And she's incredibly kind. And vulnerable. So, if someone asks to borrow something, she just gives it without a thought. Like, literally, without a thought. Because as soon as she does it, she quickly forgets that she did it. I sensed some folks were taking advantage of her condition, so we set out to address these things with her neighbors in the hopes of shutting down the back-door bank.

I got all sorts of responses. Most of the folks swore they paid it back, which we had no evidence of. But some of the responses I couldn't even follow.

"Well, it *was* a full moon, dear," one neighbor said about my mom lending her money.

Even my mom defended them. "Listen honey, we all help each out here in our little community," she said. "What do I care anyway?" she added.

Following my mom's trail of spending is a lot like being stuck in a fifth dimension where unknown forces twist and turn things around in such a way that you have no idea what things mean or how they even work any more. It's just impossible to follow at times.

"Mom, what did you write this ten-dollar check for?" my sister asked.

"Oh, that was for Joanie who needed it for Betsy, who got a basket of fruit for Bob. So, Bob gave Joanie a gallon of milk because Fred wasn't able to get to the store in time for June's birthday," she said.

Huh, we bemused.

"But Mom, how did you get your ten dollars back?" I asked.

"Oh, well I got invited to June's birthday party," she answered.

"Oh, ok," I said.

"But I didn't go because at the last minute, Fred made it a Christmas party and, well, you know how I feel about that," she added.

It turns out the retirement community is a tightly-knit group of folks with their own lingo, barter system, and code of conduct. They all cover for each other. It's like they band together to protect one another from each other's pesky grown children trying to ruin all their fun. It makes sense if you think about it. They spend most of their time together, just trying to get through the days. Children and visitors come by every so often, or in some sad cases, never. So, they rely on each other for all sorts of things. Food. Money. Companionship. Bed-side toilets, if needed. Even survival. My mom's neighbor has saved her life a few times. By simply paying attention and caring enough to take action when she needed him to.

To my sister's credit, she had been moving my mom's money around and covering for her like a nun with a gambling addiction. It was impressive, really. I finally asked about the credit card balance.

"Well, mom accidentally spent $10,000," my sister finally confessed one day.

"Oh my God, who accidentally spends $10,000?" I asked.

"Well, she can't remember what she spent it on," she said.

"We seriously don't know?" I asked.

"No, I haven't seen it," she said.

A while ago, I called my mom on a Friday evening to check on her. Seemed like the daughterly thing to do. She answered and the music in the background was so loud she could barely hear me.

"Mom!" I screamed. "Where are you?"

"Oh, I'm Up a Creek," she laughed. "We're just looking at these men who are so short and I'm going on my third drink," she was laughing hysterically.

"You're at a bar? Who are you out — wait, why are the men so short?" I asked just out of curiosity. It seemed like such a weird statement, even from my mother.

"Oh, I meant young," she clarified. "So young," she said.

"Mom, you shouldn't be out right now…" I started.

Click. She hung up on me.

Under normal circumstances, my parents are free to do what they want. The less my siblings and I know, the better. But my dad was recently diagnosed with colon cancer and, at the time of that phone call about the ladder, was just a few short weeks away from a major surgery. The colon cancer, as it turns out, explains the rolled-up telephone book in his car, "To help with the sense of urgency," he finally revealed.

And my mother, at the time she was drinking in a crowded bar, had recently been diagnosed with kidney failure and end stage liver disease.

On top of all of that, we were eight months into the COVID-19 pandemic, when being in a crowded bar could literally kill you.

20
A Sacrificial Lamb and the Irrelevance of Bodily Organs

My parents couldn't be more different. My mom loves to be pampered and wouldn't think twice about going to the spa in the middle of a deadly pandemic, just to feel pretty. She reads as if all the books in the world are going to disappear, wears a cell phone attached to a lanyard around her neck, and has no problem whipping her credit card out to pay for something. Her love language is words of affirmation because she is a genuinely kind person who loves to hear nice things said.

My dad bases his life on two seasons. Winterization and de-winterization. He is a pioneer born in the wrong century. He has never subscribed to cable television, is one hundred per cent addicted to talk radio, and pays his utility bills in person, with cash. He doesn't have a cell phone. Or a credit card. He rarely buys anything that hasn't already been purchased, and used, by someone else. If he really needs something, he figures out how to make it. My dad will tell you that love languages are fucking stupid. But if I had to guess, I'd say that his are most likely quality time at the bar, and good story telling.

They are unequivocally opposing forces that, underneath it all, seem interconnected in some weird way that has transcended time.

Before I was born, my dad strong-armed my mom into going ice sailing on the nearby lake. He constructed the sailboat himself, electing not to install any flotation devices, because, as he has said for years, "I didn't think we needed them."

Ice sailing isn't a common sport for some fairly obvious reasons. It's cold. Dangerous. And it can make or break a relationship. The story has remained consistent over the years, and it has become a family legend.

One minute my parents are sailing across the ice, and the next, my mom is completely submerged in water. As it turns out, and a fact my dad found out years later, there are three spots in the lake that never fully freeze. So, as the sailboat hit one of the soft spots in the ice, the front end crashed through the slush, and my mom slid off the boat and into the freezing water.

The thing about my mom is that not only can she not swim, but she drops like a bag of cement. I've personally experienced trying to save her from deep water and can verify that she is one hundred percent dead weight.

My dad swiftly moved into action and grabbed her by the scarf wrapped around her head. He pulled her out of the water by the scarf, which was tightly wrapped around her hair. He got her back on the boat just as his friend, who ran from shore, arrived to help. My brother and sister were sitting in the car on shore, waiting for my parents to come back from their excursion. But my mom almost didn't come back. And I almost wasn't born. My mom lost a chunk of hair that day, but she lived to tell about it. And fortunately, I am here to write about it.

*

There has been a lot written about opposing forces. You see it in science, weather, and literature. There are opposing forces just to be stationary. If you're sitting on a chair, the force of gravity pulls you down into the chair. And with equal force, the chair is pushing you back up, creating balance. Hence, your ability to stay stationary. But if the chair isn't strong enough, it can't push back with the same level of force that is pushing you down. As a result, things become unbalanced, the chair breaks, and you fall to the ground.

It's an over-simplified way of explaining a lot of complex theories. But it makes a lot of sense if you think about it.

There are also opposing forces in literature, which typically center around conflict. A character is fighting against nature, or some weather event. Boarding up their house. Collecting fresh water. Putting out wildfires. Or they are fighting against another individual or group of people. Two people fighting over a romantic partner. A protest march to boycott a decision or controversial event. Or some internal conflict occurs, whereby a character is torn between the forces of good an evil. These can all be gripping vehicles to enhance a storyline, create interest and enthusiasm, and drive home an important philosophical perspective. Potentially creating a masterpiece.

But if in any way, one of those forces strengthens or weakens, the impact of that can likely change the trajectory of a movement forward. This happens mostly because opposing forces also control the speed at which things happen. If a sun/moon synastry is in perfect balance, then all of those characteristics are shown in equal light, creating the maximum benefit to those experiencing it. But if one of those is out of balance, or otherwise absent, then one will undoubtedly feel the weight of the dominating force.

*

I say all of that to say, the yin and yang pulling between my parents over the years has kept things interesting. One was getting re-married while the other was getting divorced. One fell out of my life when the other wanted back in. And now, old age is settling in, and neither are particularly graceful at it. It has been like a never-ending game of ping pong. Just when we think things are under control, a new challenge comes at us.

*

Despite their differences, they have remained in sync on some very key things.

For example, they both hate the holidays.

"I'm cancelling Christmas and birthdays. Do you hear me? I'm done." My dad said several years ago. "Now, if you all want to get me something," he went on, "well then that is on you. But, I'm tired of all the bullshit so don't expect anything from me!" he shouted through the phone.

This all came after some drama where he sent my brother a five-dollar bill for his birthday and told him to go get a drink on him. My brother lives in an area where nothing costs five dollars. So, he bought the drink, but had to come out of his own pocket for the tax and tip. He then called my dad to tell him that he owed him a few more dollars to cover the bill.

I'm not blaming my brother for losing our cards, exactly.

But I do think that got my dad's goat.

"You're the sacrificial lamb here kid, sorry," he said to me during that phone call. But you have to know my dad and his relationship with apologies, and the English language as a whole.

My dad apologizes about as frequently as a person gets struck by lightning. It does occur, but the odds of it happening are very rare. So, in the rare instance that he says, 'sorry', it sounds more like the word 'sore' but then stretch that out for a few more syllables.

I had never been a sacrificial lamb before, and it was alarming. That he could unequivocally denounce not just a holiday, but the recognition of such an event to his own child seemed cold-hearted and soulless. I am his offspring, I thought at the time. A person who shares his DNA. It's as if he said, "You failed me, and now OFF WITH YOUR HEAD!"

*

It's possible my dad ended Christmas and birthday cards because he was frustrated that we refused to hand-write him Thank You notes and letters. That was another round of phone calls.

"What's wrong with writing a goddamn letter every once in a while?" he would shout over the phone.

"Dad, nobody is writing letters any more," I said to him. "Can we get you a cell phone so we can just text you?"

It was like I hit him in the chest with a crowbar.

"Jesus Christ! Oh, get a cell phone, huh? You all have cell phones and you never answer the goddamn things!"

To be honest, he's entirely right. I don't always answer the phone when he calls. The reason I don't always answer the phone when he calls is because over the years, I have learned how to gauge his mood by the time of day. Early morning calls are safe because he hasn't started the day yet. That's when I usually call him, on my way to work at about 6:30 AM. I call that time the sweet spot. It's right about when he wakes up and just before he has tuned into the news, or goes to the bathroom.

So, it's an easy, short call. Mid-afternoon phone calls are questionable. You just never know what he has going on. Late night phone calls could absolutely wreck you for the next few days. Mostly because he's had all day to chew on whatever he's most annoyed about.

Another reason I don't always answer when he calls is because he asks the most random questions.

I recently answered the phone and got, "Listen, kid, I have a question. Are you listening? Can you hear me OK? Where are you? In the car? At home? Why aren't you working?"

"Hi dad," I said. "I'm right here, what's up?"

"Ok, listen. Can you hear me OK?"

He is obsessed with being heard.

"Yes, I can hear you ok," I answered.

"How many organs can you lose and still live?" he asked.

"What?" I asked.

"You don't need *all* of your organs, you know that, right?" he yelled.

"Um, well, I never thought about it," I replied.

"Oh, you never thought about it," he said mocking me. "Well, I'm going to tell you, I think you could lose quite a few and still live," he finished.

Taking the bait, I replied, "Huh. Ok, which ones?"

"Well, the spleen for starters," he answered. "Who the

fuck needs a spleen?" he asked.

And so it went. A forty-minute conversation about how many organs you can lose and still live.

I hung up with my father and immediately panicked that he might, someday, be in the position to make important medical decisions for me. I pictured myself being incapacitated and a doctor rattling off the many things wrong with me, and my dad, interrupting him, saying, "She doesn't need all those organs anyway." And with his sacrificial lamb mentality and all, I wouldn't stand a chance.

*

Another time he called just to tell me the bats in his house like the south-facing wall. To know why this is important is to know that my father had been having an on-again, off-again relationship with bats for years. One time I visited him and discovered wall to wall netting hanging about a foot from the ceiling. "It keeps the bats from swooping down," he said proudly.

I hadn't heard much about the bats in a while, so I assumed he finally made peace with the whole thing and just decided to live in harmony with them. As it turns out, he'd been studying them. Analyzing their habits. Predicting their movement. He was biding his time, collecting real scientific data, until he was ready to make his move.

So, when he called to say the bats liked the south facing wall, I knew he was up to something. I could hear it in his voice. There was about to be an onslaught of bat deaths.

*

But I don't always avoid his calls.

On the last election day, I called him to say that I just voted, and that I was pretty sure I canceled his vote out. This was a long-standing argument between my mother and him. When they were married, they both went to vote, like every good married couple did in the late 1960's, and on the way out she told him who she voted for and he about lost his voice hollering about how she canceled him out. It was a huge source of contention between the two of them. So, me bringing it up was a cheap shot, I realize, but one worth taking in light of how much stuff he throws my way. He calmly rolled right over it and asked, "What year did Virginia become a Colony?"

Dammit.

Anyway, for the past ten Christmas seasons, my father has established a pretty consistent routine. As the holiday season approaches, he publicly announces his disdain for Christmas, gathers his boozy supplies, and then slumbers into hiding like a grumpy old black bear. But not before crushing every bit of joy people might be experiencing around him.

I think the thing he hates the most about the holiday season, other than watching people being joyful, is Santa Claus. He absolutely despises the idea of the guy. As kids, he never once talked about Santa Claus. He didn't spoil it for us, necessarily, but he certainly didn't buy into it at all.

"If you think I was going to spend all that money for you kids and give some other guy credit, well you got another thing coming," he said. "That's just fucking stupid," he finished.

His hatred for Santa only deepened over the years.

He started obsessively calling, even in July, furious about it all.

"Diane, listen, can you hear me?" he asked during one phone call in July.

"Yes dad, I can hear you," I replied.

"What do you think about your sister lying to her kids about Santa Claus, huh? I mean, what do you really think? You're a psychologist," he said.

"Dad, they're kids, let them believe in Santa Claus," I said.

"Well what kind of psychologist believes in lying to kids, huh?" he asked.

Sometimes, there are just not enough words, I thought at the time.

*

Because of my parents' sun/moon synastry, one of them can't not do what the other has either already done or plans to do. They are masterfully in sync like that.

When my dad eliminated Christmas and birthdays, it was actually our *second* time losing them. Because my mom had already canceled Christmas years earlier, saying the holiday tradition was just too expensive.

"Yes mom, you should absolutely spend the money on things that you need. I don't need anything," I said to her.

We were all surprised, when she sent us her Christmas wish list. When I called and asked about it her reply was quite matter of fact.

"Well, I can't afford Christmas, but that doesn't mean we all should suffer," she announced.

Another reason my mom hates the holidays, especially Christmas, is because she said that, as a kid, they always had to travel to West Virginia to visit extended family. She gets car sick, and she was always stuck in the back seat as they drove through the hills of West Virginia. That's being sick, both on the way in and on the way out. And, to make matters worse, they always drove back home the day after Christmas, which ironically is also her birthday. On top of all of that, her presents were wrapped in holiday paper and her parents would casually tell her on Christmas Morning to 'Go ahead and pick one of those for your birthday.'

She has carried this emotional trauma with her through the years, ensuring that all of her children knew it, understood it, and respond accordingly to it. Hence, why we never travelled on or around Christmas, wrapped her birthday gifts in neutral paper, and handed them to her on December 26th, and not a day sooner.

*

Another thing that my parents both agree on, and this is the key issue here, is the *perception* of how we were raised. They both will tell you things that just didn't happen. Or at least they didn't happen in the way they describe. Their perceptions are no doubt clouded by the *idea* of parenting. It's as if to say, well yes, of course we did those things in that way because that is what good parents do.

In some weird way they must have had this unwritten agreement that free-range parenting made sense. I'm not sure if it was because it was just easier, if they fundamentally believed in it, or they just didn't know any better. But nonetheless, they came to a consensus on the idea, put the ship into gear, and never once looked back.

*

My mom has studied astrology for years. When I was a kid, she belonged to an astrology club. I remember being carted off to an old farmhouse where her and some other folks would sit around, studying charts, aspects, and orbits. It teetered on fortune telling really, and after one particularly strange event that she would never talk about, she stopped going to the club.

As a result, she became a closet astrologer. As a kid, she was generally un-phased by events because she seemed to always know what was about to happen, or that she totally expected the thing to happen, because that's how the stars had been aligned.

As such, I suspect my mom had a better sense of what her three kids were doing based on charts, rather than the actual reality of it all. It's as if she knew exactly what we were likely to do, or not do, given the time and location of where she birthed us.

Even now when I'm having a bad day, I'll call her to talk about it. She listens patiently and when I'm all finished, she'll say, "Well, you know honey, your Mercury is just sitting out there all by itself."

Similarly, my father has always left little room for pity, which is another thing both of my parents have in common. Whatever your situation is, their situation is way worse.

He called one day as I was driving home from work and asked how things were going. I went into this whole story about a terrible meeting, complaining about this or that. And he listened patiently until I was all done. There was a long pause and then, "Geeze kid, I don't know. I mean, work is meant to be miserable and life sucks."

He continued, "I mean just yesterday I was knee deep in a pile of shit. Like a REAL pile of shit because I got a real bad plumbing job going on over here. Why don't you come on over here for a few days and you can get a good look at a shitty way to spend a day, huh?"

In all fairness, I don't think my parents started off like this. I don't think anyone starts off the way they eventually end up. Circumstances and perspectives change over time. Life throws lemons. Surprise obstacles. Hand grenades, even. You do the best you can in the situation. It's easy to make a wrong turn. Become lost. Hell, some people give up entirely. But when two forces unite, collectively announce, "This way," and go full throttle, it's hard to turn that ship around.

When you're young, you just go along for the ride. You don't have much of a choice in that regard. Sometimes it's a fun ride. But mostly, it's a complete shipwreck. You quickly learn that if you fall off the boat, it doesn't always turn back around for you. Not because they want to see you drown necessarily. But mostly because they simply didn't see you fall off the boat in the first place. So, as a kid, you learn to hold on real tight. Or at least become a really good swimmer.

As you get older, and as you learn more about the world and gain new skills, you attempt to take command of the ship. Steer it in a different direction. And safely sail it off into the sunset.

But still, some people double down. They disregard pleas to change course and ignore any hint that complete destruction is on the horizon. Despite the heavy seas' warnings, they remain steadfast in their navigation, blatantly shouting, "Full speed ahead!"

21
The Generations

Sifting through the generations of behavior patterns of my family in order to find balance and wellness has been a lot like living through a season of *Survivor*. I've been confronted with emotional and mental challenges that made me question my own inner strength, pitted me against others, forced me to make alliances I wouldn't normally make, and pushed me in front of the Tribal Council more times than I can count. On the worst of days, I've voted a family member off the island.

But somewhere in the midst of all of that surviving, I learned the importance of understanding, or at least being aware of, some of those patterns. Especially if I wanted to break any of those toxic cycles. I believe the work, for me at least, has been in analyzing, understanding, and breaking those patterns in order to enhance my own wellness; which as it turns out, has enabled me to be there for other young people who may be spinning out of control in their own emotional turmoil and familial patterns.

But for my siblings, it has been far more personal. They have been on their own journeys to break those patterns so the next generation — their own children — are free of them.

Either way, to fully understand my parents, it's important to understand how it all started.

If you ask my mom, I was an eager baby. And long. In

1972, I entered the world at a hospital record of 22 inches. My mom was in labor for two hours. She said I shot out like a rocket, hit the ground running, and never once looked back. According to her, I was an easy baby, an impossible toddler, and a reckless youth. Today, she will tell you I bring her the most joy. Unless my brother and sister are around; in which case, she loves us all equally.

Her parents, Gladys and Herbert, both hailed from the deep hills of West Virginia. Both families migrated to Ohio, where they eventually met. At the time, my grandmother was working at the Sears and Roebuck Company in the sewing machine department, and my grandfather was working at the steel mill. They met through mutual friends, and the rest was history. They were married until his sudden death in his late 50's.

Together grandma Gladys and grandpa Herbert shared three children and a dozen hunting beagles. Grandma claimed the kids, but not the beagles. Interestingly, after my grandfather's death, my grandmother never re-married and lived to see 80. As a kid in the 70's, I spent many afternoons at her place watching *The Andy Griffith* show on her old black and white TV. I remember her mostly sitting in a corner smoking, a habit she started at the age of nine. I used to steal her cigarette butts, put them in my pocket, take them home, then run out into the woods and smoke whatever was left of them. Seems weird now that I put that down on paper. But it's a detail I feel is relevant, mostly because it's a habit I've not fully committed to stopping. I'm told she had a beautiful voice and could do the harmonies, which landed her on a Christian public radio show when she was very young. She had a cold demeanor and fiery temper, and was known to throw a knife or two at grandpa over the years. But otherwise, she was mentally sharp up until the day she died.

Grandpa Herbert took me to my first bar. I was just a baby. He proudly propped me up on the bar and offered me little sips of soda. Apparently, I was a big hit. I was two years old when he died, but somehow remember the smell of his pipe like it was yesterday. In fact, his old rustic pipe stand and ash tray now sit next to my favorite chair at home.

I can envision what Grandpa Herbert must have looked like, driving home all boozed up, with a baby on his lap — no seatbelt or car seat — and a pipe in his mouth. His pipe smoking is a memory that I have not been able to shake over the years. Some say two years old is too young to form such a strong memory but tell that to my memory. The pipe smoke is real. And it has stuck.

*

At 78, my mom has experienced a lot of loss. She is the last surviving member of her immediate family, which seems to have spawned a dark cloud that pervasively looms over her. All told, my mom has paid for about a half dozen funerals in her life. A fact that suggests that she has been the one to mostly have it together in life. She doesn't talk a lot about her childhood, other than she was an eager to please kind of kid. And a rule follower. As such, she stood in the shadow of her siblings, who had big personalities and seemed to always stir an otherwise quiet pot.

If you ask my dad, he will tell you it was "no problem" that I was born. I remember pushing him on this very issue years ago. "But was I planned?" I asked him over and over. It has only mattered to me because my mother divorced him shortly after I was born. I essentially never knew them as a married couple. So, the timing of it all seemed relevant.

But either way, he has been steadfast in his response. "It was no problem, kid."

*

My paternal grandfather was John Ross of Niles, Ohio, formally known as John Russo. He moved to America as a boy, and his father promptly changed their last name to sound more American. Hence, Russo to Ross. He was Sicilian and he carried all the traits of a certified Italian.

There was another John Ross in the same town who was a sheriff. I would always get that question. "Oh, your grandpa the sheriff?"

"No," I would say. "My grandpa is John Ross the truck driver."

They were always short conversations. Because back then, Italian truck drivers or construction workers near Youngstown, Ohio were usually affiliated with the mafia. My grandfather certainly had the look of a mafia guy, but I can neither confirm nor deny the fact. I'll leave it as I can't confidently say he was NOT affiliated with the mafia.

My fondest memory of him occurred at the Italian American Club (ITAM). I sipped on Dago Red wine that was made in the basement. I vividly recall seeing it swirling around the glass, still trying to ferment. I watched him walk around the dark, smokey room socializing with other local Italians. He always wore khaki pants, a button down short-sleeve polo, and a fedora. Always a fedora. Short in stature but always tan and fit, he was on his game in that world. He introduced me to everyone, and they all got a huge kick out of the fact he brought his granddaughter to the ITAM. I was around 12. I think it was the day I first fell in love. Not with my grandfather necessarily, he was ok. But it was the day I discovered what an environment like that can do for your soul. The connections you make that, in a way, complete you.

I learned years later that Dago was an ethnic slur, but when I was a kid, that word was thrown in the air like pizza dough. If you walked into my grandparent's house on any given day, you would immediately be offered two choices of wine. Dago Red or Dago White. That's just what they called it.

*

My grandparents were married over fifty years. They met in the 1920's at the Cortland Roller Rink. He was, what they called back then, a skate boy. As my dad tells it, "He put roller skates on a lot of pretty girls."

Like a lot of Italian immigrant guys during that time, he dropped out of the ninth grade to work. He hustled all sorts of jobs. The skate boy turned into a landscaper and eventual business owner and truck driver. As my dad tells it, "He was driving a tractor one day and opening an ice cream stand the next." Followed by, "He sold the ice cream stand and bought a motel." It was a time when you could do such things, without any formal education, and still manage to raise and support a family of five.

*

My grandmother was Finnish but made a pizza that even the Italians loved. She had a jealous streak in her and turned the discovery of a random knee-high stocking into a three-year battle with my grandfather. The story of the knee-high stocking was that is just mysteriously appeared one day in the house. And it wasn't hers. It sat on their kitchen table for years. Anyone who came into the house was questioned about the stocking. A suspect, even. She methodically worked through a variety of possible sources, but she always came back to grandpa. He seemed to enjoy the attention. She would be interrogating visitors while they ate a slice of her freshly made pizza and he would walk in, hear the conversation, then walk off chuckling.

Irene, my grandmother was not a warm and fuzzy grandma. She wasn't going to knit you any hats or rub your back if you were sick. She would likely hand you a $20 bill as you walked out the door or ask you to stay away entirely if you had a cold. She died of lung cancer at 72, though she never smoked a day in her life. My grandfather followed her about six months later. The story of the mysterious stocking died with them.

I had the pleasure of knowing my great-grandmother, my dad's grandma. She was an interesting lady. She had a light brown curly haired wig that made her look 30 years younger. She wore a classic housecoat everywhere she went. And she carried a handbag like the Queen of England. She took a liking to me and offered to watch me when nobody else could. I don't know if she was completely up for the job, given her age at the time and the fact I was notorious for not listening to anyone.

But I listened to my great grandma. Mostly because she scared the hell out of me. She had a small old house that had a trap-door basement. The house was something out of the 1800's. Whenever I was dropped off there, I was afraid to move anywhere because of the ghosts. I was sure there were ghosts in her house. And I was terrified of the trap door that led to the basement, where I thought dead people were buried. She was the only person who told me to, "Sit right there and don't move," and I did exactly what she said.

Family legend has it that she murdered a litter of kittens one time using a couple of knee-high stockings. Stuffed the little guys in there and then beat them to death.

"That's just what they did back then, kid," my dad said squinting his eyes and shaking his head thinking about it.

"Is it though?" I asked skeptically.

My dad was really good about visiting her, and that became a regular stop on our Sunday visitation day. Probably my favorite memory of my great-grandmother occurred during a notorious Northeast Ohio snowstorm. We rolled up to her old house, just to, "Take her out for a spin."

My dad drove us all over the empty snow-covered roads of our small town, sliding through stop signs and doing full on donuts in the middle of intersections. I was sandwiched between the two of them in the front seat of his old Buick Lesabre, just slamming into them with each erratic turn. No seatbelts. She laughed and laughed, shouting, "Oh Gary!" trying desperately to hold onto her handbag.

I was sad when she died. They didn't let me go to the funeral because I was too young. But I would have liked to have gone. At least to try to find out more about the ghosts and dead people.

As a kid, my dad said nobody ever knew where he was. He was usually out fishing, building boats out of timber, or getting into alley fights with the neighborhood kids. He describes his parents as emotionally distant, which was just fine with him. When talking about his childhood, he always gives off the vibe that he didn't really *need* his parents. They were there, sure. But it's like he was born grown up. He could just do things. He got lost in his world of history books, his favorite dog Rinney, and trying a hundred different ways to get on the water. He loved the freedom he had as a kid and I think he wanted that for his own kids.

22
Stopping the Gene

My mother could have been a corporate executive with her work ethic and leadership skills in the office. At the height of her career, world renown doctors listened to what she had to say because she managed their medical credentials. She frequently told them what to do and when. And they listened. Or they couldn't practice. A powerful role if you think about it.

Those days are long gone. Now, she can become easily confused. But her stubbornness and sarcasm shine through. When I hand her the medicine she absolutely hates, she holds it high, and says, "Bottoms up." She's never been a big drinker, at least by my definition, but she's been known to hide a few small bottles of Fireball in her bra. And coins, too, now that I think about it. When I was a kid, I used to tease her that she was going to have 'In God We Trust' imprinted on her boob.

Not long ago, she told me that her mother warned her that the third child would bring a great deal of stress because you only have two hands and three kids. "One is always going to feel left out," my grandmother said to her almost fifty years ago. My mom told me she never had to worry about that because, even though I was the third child, I never wanted to hold her hand. I was too busy running. And, as it turns out, when you're too busy running, you miss out on all of the important stuff a kid needs to develop social-emotional skills. Like making emotional connections, developing positive relationships, understanding social norms, showing empathy and compassion for others, and learning how to resolve conflicts constructively. It's so much more than just holding hands.

It's not to say she didn't *try* to create those opportunities. When I was little, she set aside special time for just the two of us, which wasn't easy with her work schedule. She took me to the store in hopes I'd be interested in clothing other than my favorite Incredible Hulk T-shirt, which I wore day-after-day. But I couldn't be bothered with clothes. I ran away from her in the stores. Hung on the clothes racks. Refused to leave the toy aisle.

I missed out on all of those important things because, the truth is, we were just trying to survive. When you're in constant motion, living in perpetual chaos, and just trying to survive from one day to the next, that level of bonding and skill development takes a back seat. The neural pathways in the brain get blocked. So, the fact that our relationship seemed eerily void of any kind of emotional connection makes sense if you think about it, because I was always twenty steps ahead of her.

*

About a year ago, I could see the fear of death in my father's eyes. It was palpable. He took to organizing his otherwise chaotic life. Got his affairs in order. Sent us all letters in the mail. And then he started talking in code. He brought up the bats again, and how they liked the south-facing walls. "They just like to dig right in and hope for the best," he said.

Out of the blue, I heard a story about a town donkey being buried alive and how he escaped. "You shake it off and step up. You hear me kid?" he asked.

Are these last pieces of parenting advice? Or clues to where something is buried in his house?

I simply have no idea.

To be honest, my father's creativity and commentary talents were wasted in the factory where he worked for 30 years. He can turn anything into a good story. He should have been a history teacher, a major news broadcaster, or the host of his own radio show. I remember sitting on the dock at the boat ramp all those years ago, listening to him narrate the chaos in front of us. I was mesmerized by his perspective and comedic timing. And completely engrossed in his ability to capture the moment so precisely. They weren't just boaters. They were his people. They weren't just situations. They were life events. And we weren't just watching them. We were living it right along with them.

My father is a complicated guy. He's charismatic and funny as hell. But he's also difficult. Abrasive. He pushed us in ways you'll never find in *'How to Parent'* books.

When we were kids, he used his open hand to clip us upside the head when we made a careless mistake. If you think about it, making careless mistakes is kind of the thing kids are most known for. Over time, clipping became part of our family culture. We learned to expect it. If I dropped something in front of him, I instinctively ducked my head, and then bent over to pick the thing up. If I botched throwing him a water ski in the water, I'd hear, "I'm gonna' clip you upside the head when I get back in that boat." Sometimes he clipped us for no reason, saying, "That's for something you did when I wasn't around."

*

Now, he is in limbo. Stuck somewhere between illness and recovery. When I talk with him, there's a weakness in his voice. He has shed the muscles I most remember as a kid. He is thin. Frail, even. He's taken to holding his pants up with a bungee cord. "For quick release," he told me the other day.

He's making a hell of a go at life right now, with the help of his life partner. Or, as my dad calls her, his 'backup.' She's the same person who abandoned us in a fitful rage at a remote campground all those years ago. She left us a thousand miles from home and vulnerable to the elements. But now, she is working hard to keep him alive and well, which, we've discovered, is not an easy task.

Having the opportunity to get to know my father over the years, I can honestly say that maybe he deserved that level of desertion. That maybe I would have done the same thing in the moment because he's the kind of guy that can take you to that level of rage. I see her differently now than I did forty years ago, because I understand what she has been up against all these years. She has hung in there when most would have jumped ship. We are grateful for that, and the care she gives him.

To be 80 years old in the middle of a global pandemic must be like living on Mars. Everything is foreign and life is uncertain. A deadly virus lingers outside of your front door. But he has not lost his sense of humor, and his stubbornness remains strong.

I recently picked him up from the hospital after invasive

colon cancer surgery. He was standing on the curb holding a small overnight bag, waving like Forest Gump.

"I'm coming home with an unexpected gift," he said in the car on the way home.

"What's that?" I asked.

"My balls are five times larger than when I went in," he said laughing.

This led to fifty minutes of testicle jokes, which is forty-nine minutes longer than necessary.

He is 80, and his recovery from the surgery is slow and painful.

"Dad, call the doctor to make sure this is how you're supposed to feel," I pleaded with him.

"I ain't there yet, kid," he said stubbornly.

*

But I am there. I've been there for a long time now. I've been in the place where it's ok to ask a professional if this is how one is supposed to feel about something. I like to know these things. I've come to rely on these things for my own wellness. And sanity.

I also learned that I wasn't crazy for carrying around all that hostility because you essentially feel how you feel, and there's no right or wrong with that. I discovered, with some help, that I just hadn't thoroughly processed it all and stepped back enough to see it from a different perspective. That changing your perspective could change how you feel about a situation. Change the course of your life, even.

*

But mostly, I learned that normal is subjective. What is one person's normal is another's dysfunction. And the reverse can also be true. For example, I happen to think a morning whiskey gets the day going in the right direction. Other people may think that sounds a lot like a problem. My wife's family goes overboard on buying Christmas gifts for each other. They also spend an inordinate amount of time together over the holidays. That is their holiday norm and they love every minute of it. I think it's silly to spend so much money for each other when everyone is gainfully employed, and they can just buy stuff for themselves whenever they want. She says I don't have any holiday spirit. I say it's weird to like your family that much.

*

In retrospect, I had parents who gave me the space to be free. They fostered my creativity and allowed me to be the kind of kid I *needed* to be. It wasn't always ok to do the things I did, and they let me know about it, for sure. But it was ok to be who I was, free from judgement, and without being held to some unattainable standard. They assumed I needed to be that way; as was the case for how they, themselves, needed to be. Free to parent in a way that worked for them.

I've come to learn that overcoming resentments, resolving conflicts, and making peace with any lasting consequences of my free-range childhood has been a lot like trying to follow a treasure map. It's been a slow go. Mostly because I have no sense of direction. But also, because each new clue seems to take me down some strange rabbit hole that I can't find my way out of.

*

I am a rational person driven largely by what makes sense in the moment. Think first, put uncomfortable things into their respective places, and then feel. But only if absolutely necessary. As such, it takes all the energy I have to be present for my parents when they need me the most. Present in a way that they were not able to be for me when I needed them the most.

The truth is, I learned how to be present by working with kids. I mean kids with real emotional and psychological challenges. Those kinds of kids taught me the beauty of raw emotion and unfiltered rage. That no matter how emotionally damaged you feel, with some work, emotional growth is possible. Because of them, I learned how to sit in chaos, find my breath, and lean into the discomfort.

For me, working with kids was a lot like coming home. They gave me a purpose. I finally stopped running and rooted into the ground like a growing tree, absorbing all the nutrients I could find. I developed my own emotional vocabulary through research and lesson plans, and I incorporated those concepts into my classroom. I worked hard to establish trust with my students, show vulnerability when appropriate, and build relationships accordingly. It was like I was an adult student in my own classroom, and we were all on the social-emotional pilgrimage together.

Once I figured it all out at work, I then incorporated those philosophies into my personal life. Did the work. Opened old compartments and released all my Denial Files out into the universe. An enormous weight was lifted. Walls crumbled down. Neural pathways became unblocked and new connections began to form. I finally allowed myself to love and be loved.

I'm working hard to get to the place where it is ok to just *be*. And to understand that things just *are*. Free from judgement and outside influences. I'm close. Almost there. Some days are better than others. I long to find the kind of balance that allows me to rest comfortably in between these two opposing forces. Entirely neutral. Still. And peaceful.

Whether I ever achieve that level of peace or not, I feel profoundly grateful for this gift of time and opportunity. As in, the time I've been able to spend with my parents in their twilight years, and the opportunity to set aside past grievances so that I can *see* them in a way I never have before. To be present in a way that I never thought possible. To laugh, shake my head, and bask in the absurdity of it all. Because every time I feel like we have a grip on things, a fall happens and a shoulder gets broken. One more challenge to navigate.

I am acutely aware, though, that at any moment, an entire world can disappear. And for that, I recognize that we are all human. Inherently Flawed. And entirely vulnerable.

*

Deep into their twilight years, my parents are drifting in and out of reality, pausing, on occasion to drop anchor long enough to collect their thoughts. Reflect, even. And I've grown tired of running, which is good because they're not able to chase me any more. So, we are just sitting in it, and getting through it, *together*.

*

I'd like to think that nothing could surprise me at this point.

That we've exhausted the scope of all possible scenarios. But still, the things they say sometimes.

"No one is more surprised by your success than I am," my dad said to me recently.

"What does that even mean?" I asked.

*

My father has always asked the profound question, "What good are genes if you can't pass them on?"

It's a fair question, though I can't help but wonder, *all* the genes? Surely, I think, there are some we should stop.

For example, orangutan arms. We all have them. Sleeves are always too short and there's just nowhere to comfortably rest your arms in a way that doesn't make it look like you are about to take off on a foot race. They are inconvenient, for sure. But also, surprisingly useful for changing lightbulbs and plucking things out of those hard-to-reach places.

The clipping gene can go. Instilling an innate fear of being randomly smacked upside the head for no good reason seems inherently useless. Abusive, even. The fear of a clip doesn't make a person any less clumsy. I can't reference any scientific data on this, but it seems fairly obvious.

*

I say all of that to say, three out of the five of us have evolved. Matured. Gained a greater perspective on life. My brother and sister are well-established. Successful, even. They have each put two kids through college, which required a great deal of sacrifice. They have worked diligently to provide for their kids; to give them everything they've ever needed to be successful. They put off vacations and big purchases. Stayed in stressful jobs just to have quality health insurance for their kids.

My brother and sister showed up for their kids in ways our own parents didn't show up for us. They had regular family dinners. Attended after-school activities. And became involved in church events. And much like our younger years, they have paved the way for me to be able to live my most authentic and free-spirited life, for which I am forever grateful. I am in awe of their unwavering commitment to their families and long-term marriages; 28 — and 25-years, respectfully. A real feat in our family.

I have three nieces and one nephew, all college graduates on their way to becoming the next generation of normal, and a more improved version of us. They are already amazing. Grounded. And kind. They understand their roots and watched their parents work hard so they could have a better life. To my knowledge, none of them have ever had to climb through a bedroom window to get in the house after school.

They experienced the best their parents had to offer. Though, I suspect if you ask each of them, separately, if they had normal parents, they would likely laugh and respond with a resounding 'No!' And then immediately outline the myriad of crazy things they did to them. But as far as I can tell, none of them are nearly as crazy as the things our parents did to us.

And the same is also true for my parents. My dad will tell you his father never did much with him. They never went camping. That he was essentially left alone to figure life out. I'm guessing that influenced the kind of father he ultimately became, because my dad was around, took us places, and made a point to have an impact on us. But he also made sure we understood life wasn't going to be easy. That we had to work hard for everything.

My mom may have missed a few important *mom* moments, but she never took to throwing knives around like her mom did. I suspect growing up with a mom who had a fiery temper probably influenced the kind of mom she ultimately became.

*

At the end of the day, my nieces and nephew have enjoyed good grandparents, because, as it turns out, my parents are way better at *grand*parenting. In turn, they will eventually have their own children and raise them to push through even more barriers and achieve greater levels of success than my great-grandparents ever thought possible for a family from such humble beginnings. And their children will have children, and with each subsequent generation, they will have the opportunity to establish a new level of normal. After all, that's how generations are supposed to work.

As for me, the genes stop here. Without any children of my own, I've done my part to prevent future generations of dysfunction. To end the cycle of madness. Nail the coffin shut. And I feel pretty good about all of that because this story is my legacy now. And just as my grandparents survived their parents, and my parents survived their parents, I'm surviving my own parents. Though, I'd like to think I'm doing more than just surviving. I'd like to believe that I'm thriving. Enlightened, even. That I've evolved into this first generation of normal. Not too bad for a sacrificial lamb.

The End